Tuscany Travel Guide

2025

A Step-by-step Complete Book to Discovering the Top Attractions and Hidden Gems with Recommended Itineraries and Detailed Maps.

La Lunigiana

Garfagnana

Carrara
Massa

Pietrasanta
Lucca

Firenze
(Florence)

San
Miniato

Greve

Chianti
Classico

San Gimignano

Volterra

Siena

Cortona

Crete Senese

Montepulciano

Massa
Marittima

Pienza

Montalcino

Elba

Maremma

Grosseto

Monte
Argentario

Tuscany

Historic Territories

More detailed maps in the maps section

Contents

Introduction

A Warm Tuscan Welcome

Tuscany is more than a destination; it's a state of

mind. As you step onto its sunlit soil, a warm

embrace of history, culture, and beauty greets you. Here, life slows down, and every moment feels purposeful. The golden hills, the cypress trees standing tall like ancient sentinels, and the melody of church bells echoing through medieval towns—it's all part of Tuscany's magic.

For decades, I have wandered these lands, not as a tourist but as a lifelong student of its charm. Each village whispers stories of the past, and every meal carries the essence of generations. Tuscany invites you to savor life's simplest joys: a sip of Chianti under the shade of an olive tree, a stroll through cobblestone streets where time seems to stand still, or a hearty bowl of ribollita at a family-run trattoria.

In this book, I aim to bring you not just the must-sees but the heart of Tuscany—the places where locals gather, where traditions thrive, and where the true spirit of the region shines. So, whether you're a first-time visitor or returning for the umpteenth time, know that Tuscany always has something new to offer. Let's discover its wonders together.

My Decades of Tuscan Wanderings

I first set foot in Tuscany over four decades ago, and I've been under its spell ever since. Back then, it was a quieter place, less touched by the hum of modern tourism. I remember wandering the rolling hills of Chianti with little more than a map and a sense of wonder, stopping in small villages where English was rare but hospitality was abundant.

Over the years, I've watched Tuscany evolve. Florence grew into a bustling hub of art lovers, while once-hidden gems like Val d'Orcia became celebrated for their breathtaking landscapes. Yet, what has always struck me is how Tuscany remains deeply rooted in its traditions. Families still gather to make wine the old-fashioned way, artisans craft leather goods with techniques passed down through generations, and the local festivals—oh, the festivals!—continue to bring communities together.

I've walked the vineyards of Montepulciano at sunrise, tasted pecorino cheese in Pienza while chatting with its makers, and marveled at the frescoes in Arezzo as if seeing them for the first time. Each visit, each encounter, has deepened my love for this region. This book is my attempt to share those experiences with you, to guide you through the Tuscany I've come to know so well.

Why Tuscany Beckons in 2025

Tuscany in 2025 is a vibrant blend of timeless beauty and contemporary appeal. While its historic towns and countryside remain largely unchanged, this year brings fresh opportunities to experience the region like never before.

The post-pandemic era has seen Tuscany embrace a slower, more sustainable form of tourism. New agriturismos (farm stays) offer intimate settings where you can immerse yourself in rural life, learning to make pasta or harvest olives alongside local families. Vineyards are experimenting with organic and biodynamic winemaking, inviting visitors to taste wines that reflect the land's purity.

Technology has also enhanced the experience without detracting from its charm. Guided tours now use augmented reality to bring history to life, letting you see Florence as it appeared in

Michelangelo's time. Meanwhile, lesser-known towns are making a name for themselves with art exhibitions, culinary festivals, and boutique accommodations.

What truly sets Tuscany apart in 2025 is its enduring spirit. It's a place where the old and new coexist seamlessly, where you can spend the morning exploring a medieval fortress and the afternoon savoring a modern twist on classic Tuscan cuisine. Tuscany beckons not just for its sights but for its way of life—a reminder to slow down, savor the moment, and connect with something greater than yourself.

This year, more than ever, Tuscany invites you to discover its treasures, both ancient and new. Whether you're drawn by its art, its landscapes, or its food, I promise you'll leave with a piece of Tuscany etched into your heart.

Chapter 1: Tuscany Through the Ages

Ancient Roots: From Etruscans to Romans

Tuscany's story begins long before the Roman Empire or the bustling cities we know today. Thousands of years ago, the Etruscans ruled this land, shaping its culture and identity. These mysterious people, who lived here from around 800 BC, were skilled farmers, traders, and artisans. They didn't leave behind as many written records as the Greeks or Romans, but their influence on Tuscany is undeniable.

The Etruscans built their towns on hilltops for defense, many of which evolved into the towns we visit today. Cortona, Volterra, and Fiesole were once thriving Etruscan settlements. As you walk through their cobbled streets, it's easy to imagine life back then—markets bustling with trade, temples where rituals were performed, and homes adorned with intricate pottery. The Etruscans were masters of terracotta and gold, and you can still see their craftsmanship in museums like the Guarnacci Museum in Volterra.

When the Romans arrived in the 3rd century BC, they didn't erase Etruscan culture but absorbed it. They brought new infrastructure, building roads, aqueducts, and towns like Florence, which began as a Roman military camp. The Romans appreciated Tuscany for its fertile land and mild climate, using it to grow wheat, olives, and grapes—the very foundation of today's Tuscan cuisine.

Yet, even as the Romans expanded their empire, the Etruscan spirit endured. Their language, though largely lost, influenced Latin, and their reverence for nature shaped the way the land was cultivated. Tuscany today remains a place where the past feels alive, and the legacy of the Etruscans and Romans is woven into its very fabric.

The Renaissance Awakening: Art, Science, and Legacy

If the Etruscans laid the groundwork for Tuscany, the Renaissance was its crowning achievement. Beginning in the 14th century, this period saw Tuscany, particularly Florence, become the cultural and intellectual heart of Europe. It was a time of extraordinary creativity, when art, science, and philosophy flourished as never before.

Florence was the epicenter of it all. The Medici family, wealthy bankers and patrons of the arts, played a key role in fostering this golden age. They supported geniuses like Leonardo da Vinci, Michelangelo, and Botticelli, whose works still draw millions of visitors each year. Imagine Michelangelo chiseling away at his David in a Florentine workshop or Botticelli painting "The Birth of Venus" in the Medici's palace.

But the Renaissance wasn't just about art. It was a time of scientific breakthroughs as well. Galileo Galilei, born in Pisa, revolutionized our understanding of the universe with his studies of astronomy and physics. His work laid the foundation for modern science, challenging old beliefs and inspiring future generations.

Tuscany also saw a revival in architecture during this period. The dome of Florence's Cathedral, designed by Filippo Brunelleschi, was an engineering marvel of its time and remains one of the most iconic symbols of the Renaissance. Meanwhile, towns like Siena and Lucca preserved their medieval charm while embracing the artistic spirit of the era.

The Renaissance left an indelible mark on Tuscany. Its art, architecture, and ideas continue to inspire, reminding us of what humanity can achieve when creativity and curiosity are nurtured. As you explore Tuscany, you'll feel the echoes of this incredible era in every corner.

Modern Tuscany: Where Tradition Meets Innovation

Tuscany today is a harmonious blend of old and new. While its roots stretch deep into history, the region has embraced modernity in ways that enhance, rather than diminish, its timeless appeal. This balance is one of the reasons why Tuscany remains so captivating.

Take agriculture, for example. Tuscany's vineyards and olive groves are centuries old, but many farmers are now adopting sustainable practices. Organic and biodynamic farming methods are becoming the norm, ensuring that the land remains fertile for future generations. You'll find wineries where traditional techniques meet modern technology, producing wines that are both authentic and innovative.

The region's culinary scene mirrors this approach. While traditional dishes like pappardelle al cinghiale (wild boar pasta) and ribollita (Tuscan bread soup) are still celebrated, contemporary chefs are reimagining these classics. They're blending local ingredients with global flavors, creating a dining experience that's both rooted in tradition and excitingly modern.

Art and culture in Tuscany have also evolved. While the masterpieces of the Renaissance draw visitors to galleries and churches, contemporary artists are leaving their mark too. Cities like Florence and Pisa host modern art exhibitions and installations, showcasing the talents of today's creative minds.

Technology has also played a role in shaping modern Tuscany. From eco-friendly accommodations to guided tours using augmented reality, the region has found ways to enhance the travel experience without losing its soul. Yet, amidst all these advancements, Tuscany's core values remain unchanged: a deep respect for the land, a love of community, and an appreciation for life's simple pleasures.

As you explore Tuscany in 2025, you'll see how its history and modernity coexist beautifully. It's a place where the past isn't just remembered but celebrated, and where innovation is embraced without compromising what makes Tuscany truly special.

Artistic Marvels: The Duomo, Uffizi, and Beyond

When people think of Florence, they often think of art—and for good reason. Florence is the birthplace of the Renaissance, and its streets are like an open-air museum, brimming with creativity and history. Nowhere is this more evident than in its artistic landmarks, starting with the iconic Duomo.

The Cathedral of Santa Maria del Fiore, affectionately called the Duomo, is Florence's crown jewel. Its massive red-tiled dome, designed by Filippo Brunelleschi in the 15th century, dominates the skyline. Standing beneath this architectural marvel, it's hard not to feel awe. Climb to the top if you're able—the view of Florence from there is breathtaking. Inside, the cathedral's frescoed dome, painted by Giorgio Vasari and Federico Zuccari, tells stories of heaven and hell in vivid detail.

Just a short walk away is the Uffizi Gallery, home to some of the world's most famous artworks. Step inside, and you'll find masterpieces like Botticelli's The Birth of Venus and da Vinci's Annunciation. Walking through the Uffizi is like flipping through the pages of an art history book, with each room offering another chapter of brilliance. If you plan to visit, reserve your tickets in advance—the Uffizi is popular for a reason.

Beyond these two landmarks, Florence's artistic treasures are seemingly endless. Michelangelo's David at the Accademia Gallery draws crowds daily, while the Palazzo Pitti offers a glimpse into the grandeur of the Medici family. Even the city's churches, like Santa Croce and San Lorenzo, are filled with art. Florence is a place where creativity lives in every corner, and exploring its artistic marvels is an unforgettable journey.

Chapter 2: Florence – Cradle of the Renaissance

Florence's Culinary Scene: Traditional and Modern

When it comes to food, Florence knows how to impress. The city's culinary traditions are as rich as its history, and its chefs have mastered the art of turning simple ingredients into unforgettable meals.

Florentine cuisine is rooted in simplicity. It relies on fresh, local ingredients and time-honored recipes. Take bistecca alla Fiorentina, for instance. This massive T-bone steak, grilled over an open flame and seasoned with just salt, pepper, and olive oil, is a true Florentine classic. Pair it with a glass of Chianti, and you have a meal fit for royalty.

Another staple is ribollita, a hearty soup made with bread, beans, and vegetables. It's a dish born out of frugality, yet its flavors are anything but plain. You'll find it in trattorias all over the city, each with its own twist on the recipe. And let's not forget gelato—Florence is the birthplace of this creamy delight, and spots like Vivoli and

Gelateria dei Neri serve some of the best you'll ever taste.

While tradition is celebrated, Florence also embraces modern culinary trends. Innovative chefs are blending classic Tuscan flavors with global influences, creating dishes that are both nostalgic and exciting. Restaurants like La Bottega del Buon Caffè and Ora d'Aria offer Michelin-starred experiences that push the boundaries of Italian cuisine.

Whether you're dining in a centuries-old trattoria or trying something new at a contemporary eatery, Florence's food scene is a feast for the senses.

Local Markets: Craftsmanship and Culture

Florence's markets are more than just places to shop—they're windows into the city's soul. From bustling food stalls to artisan workshops, the markets offer a glimpse of Florence's vibrant culture and craftsmanship.

Start your journey at the Mercato Centrale, located in the San Lorenzo district. The ground floor is a food lover's paradise, with vendors selling everything from fresh produce to cured meats and cheeses. Pick up some pecorino Toscano or a slice of prosciutto and create your own picnic. Upstairs, the market transforms into a modern food court, where you can enjoy everything from wood-fired pizza to seafood pasta.

For those interested in leather goods, the San Lorenzo Market is a must-visit. Florence is famous for its leather craftsmanship, and this market is filled with stalls selling jackets, bags, and belts. While browsing, remember to check for quality—authentic Florentine leather is soft, durable, and has a distinctive smell.

Artisanship is also alive and well at the Oltrarno district's markets. Here, you'll find workshops where craftsmen create everything from jewelry to marbled paper. Visit the Santo Spirito Market for handmade goods or explore Via Maggio for antique treasures.

Finally, the Sant'Ambrogio Market offers a more local experience. Less touristy than Mercato Centrale, this market is where Florentines shop for their daily needs. Stroll through its aisles, and you'll see colorful produce, fresh fish, and even household items. It's the perfect spot to immerse yourself in Florence's daily life.

The markets of Florence aren't just places to buy things—they're where you can feel the heartbeat of the city. Take your time, soak in the atmosphere, and discover the stories behind the goods.

Chapter 3: Siena – The Medieval Jewel

The Palio and Piazza del Campo

Siena, with its medieval charm, comes alive like no other during the Palio di Siena. This thrilling horse race, held twice each summer, is not just a competition—it's the beating heart of the city's culture and identity. Picture this: thousands of spectators packed into the Piazza del Campo, Siena's grand and shell-shaped square, as ten riders representing different city districts, or contrade, compete in a race that lasts just 90 seconds.

The Palio dates back to the 17th century, though its roots go even deeper. It's more than a race; it's a showcase of Siena's passion, pride, and history. Each contrada is like a close-knit family, complete with its own colors, emblems, and rivalries. The excitement begins weeks before the race with blessings for the horses in local churches and lively parades featuring traditional costumes and banners.

The race itself is pure adrenaline. Horses gallop around the piazza's uneven, sloped surface, cheered on by passionate crowds. The riders, often bareback, do whatever it takes to win, and it's not uncommon for riderless horses to cross the finish line first. Victory brings immense pride and a year of bragging rights for the winning contrada.

Even if you're not in Siena for the Palio, the Piazza del Campo is worth visiting. Its unique shape and brick pavement are surrounded by stunning medieval buildings, including the Palazzo Pubblico and the towering Torre del Mangia. Whether you're sipping a coffee at one of the cafes or imagining the roar of the Palio crowd, the piazza is a place where Siena's history comes to life.

Gothic Wonders: Duomo di Siena

Siena's Duomo, or Cathedral, is a masterpiece of Gothic architecture that leaves visitors in awe. Built between the 12th and 14th centuries, it's a testament to the city's ambition and artistic prowess. From its striking black-and-white marble façade to its intricate interiors, the Duomo is a treasure trove of history and beauty.

The first thing you'll notice is the cathedral's exterior. Its black and white stripes, made from local marble, symbolize Siena's colors and give the building a unique appearance. The façade is adorned with sculptures, gargoyles, and intricate carvings that tell biblical stories. Lorenzo Maitani and Giovanni Pisano, two of the most skilled architects of their time, contributed to this stunning work of art.

Step inside, and you'll be greeted by an equally impressive sight. The striped theme continues on the columns, creating a sense of harmony and grandeur. The floor is a mosaic of inlaid marble panels depicting biblical scenes, allegories, and historical events. These panels are covered for most of the year to preserve them, but during certain months, they're unveiled for visitors to admire.

One of the cathedral's highlights is the Piccolomini Library, a room filled with vibrant frescoes by Pinturicchio. These frescoes celebrate the life of Pope Pius II, a native of Siena, and are accompanied by a collection of ancient manuscripts. The Duomo also houses sculptures by Michelangelo and Bernini, as well as the stunning Rose Window, which floods the interior with colored light.

The adjoining Baptistery and Museo dell'Opera del Duomo are worth exploring as well. The Baptistery features a magnificent baptismal font by Jacopo della Quercia, while the museum offers panoramic views of Siena from its rooftop terrace. The Duomo di Siena is more than a church; it's a symbol of the city's faith, creativity, and legacy.

Exploring Siena's Hidden Alleys

While the Palio and Duomo attract most of Siena's visitors, the city's charm truly reveals itself in its hidden alleys. Step away from the bustling Piazza del Campo and main tourist spots, and you'll discover a maze of narrow streets, quiet courtyards, and unexpected views that feel like stepping back in time.

Siena's alleys are full of surprises. One moment you're walking along a shaded, cobblestone street; the next, you're greeted by a breathtaking view of rolling Tuscan hills. Many of these alleys retain their medieval character, with arched doorways, terracotta rooftops, and ivy-covered walls. Wander without a plan, and you'll find charming details like wrought-iron lanterns, small shrines, and painted tiles marking the boundaries of the city's contrade.

The Contrada dell'Onda, for example, is known for its nautical-themed emblems and fountains, while the Contrada della Torre boasts some of the city's most picturesque corners. These neighborhoods are deeply tied to Siena's history and traditions, and exploring them feels like uncovering a living museum.

Hidden gems abound, such as the Fontebranda, one of Siena's oldest and most beautiful fountains. Built in the 13th century, it once provided water for the city and is tied to the story of Saint Catherine of Siena, who grew up nearby. Another secret spot is the Vicolo delle Scotte, a quiet alley that leads to the former hospital of Santa Maria della Scala, now a museum showcasing centuries of Sienese history.

For those willing to venture a little farther, the Orto de' Pecci offers a peaceful escape. This garden, located just outside the city walls, is a haven of greenery where locals relax and enjoy picnics. From here, you'll get stunning views of Siena's skyline, with the Duomo and Torre del Mangia rising above the rooftops.

Exploring Siena's hidden alleys is like peeling back the layers of a story. Each corner holds a piece of the city's soul, waiting to be discovered by those who take the time to look. It's in these quiet moments that Siena's true magic comes to life.

Chapter 4: Chianti – A Wine Lover's Paradise

Vineyards and Tastings: Must-Visit Wineries

Chianti, with its rolling hills covered in vineyards, is a paradise for wine lovers. The region is renowned for its Chianti Classico wine, a robust red made primarily from Sangiovese grapes. The black rooster on the label guarantees authenticity and quality, a mark of pride for this historic wine region.

To truly experience Chianti, a visit to its wineries is a must. Many estates are family-run and offer guided tours, tastings, and a chance to learn about their winemaking traditions. Here are some must-visit wineries:

1. Castello di Brolio

One of Chianti's oldest and most iconic wineries, Castello di Brolio, has been producing wine since the 12th century. This majestic castle offers breathtaking views of the countryside and an in-depth look at the winemaking process. Their cellar tours end with tastings of award-winning wines, including their flagship Chianti Classico Riserva.

2. Antinori nel Chianti Classico

The Antinori family has been making wine for over 600 years, and their modern winery in Bargino is a blend of tradition and innovation. The state-of-the-art facility is built into a hillside and provides immersive tours that highlight their sustainable practices. Don't miss their Chianti Classico Gran Selezione—it's a masterpiece.

3. Badia a Coltibuono

Translated as the "Abbey of Good Harvest," this 1,000-year-old monastery turned winery is a serene retreat. Guests can explore the ancient cellars, taste organic wines, and even stay overnight. Their cooking classes, paired with wine tastings, offer a full Tuscan experience.

4. Castello di Ama

Known for combining art and wine, Castello di Ama features contemporary art installations throughout the estate. Their wines are equally impressive, particularly their Chianti Classico and Merlot blends. A visit here feels like stepping into a living museum.

5. Fonterutoli

Owned by the Mazzei family for 24 generations, this winery in Castellina in Chianti is a testament to heritage. Their wine shop and enoteca are perfect for sampling their extensive range of wines, from classic reds to experimental blends.

Whether you're a wine connoisseur or a casual enthusiast, Chianti's wineries offer an unforgettable journey through Tuscany's wine culture.

The Art of Olive Oil: Liquid Gold of Tuscany

While Chianti is famous for its wine, its olive oil is equally exceptional. Known as "liquid gold," Tuscan olive oil is prized for its fruity, slightly peppery flavor and health benefits. Producing olive oil in Chianti is an art that dates back centuries, and visiting an olive mill is an enlightening experience.

The region's hilly terrain and mild climate create ideal conditions for olive cultivation. Most olive oils here are extra virgin, the highest quality grade, made by cold-pressing olives without chemicals. The result is a pure, flavorful oil that's perfect for drizzling over bruschetta, salads, or even a simple slice of bread.

Olive Harvest and Production

The olive harvest in Chianti typically takes place in late October and early November. Farmers hand-pick the olives to ensure they're handled gently and rushed to the mill for pressing. This minimizes oxidation and preserves the oil's fresh taste and nutrients.

Visiting an olive mill, such as Fattoria La Vialla or Frantoio di Santa Téa, is a fascinating way to learn about the process. Many mills offer guided tours where you can see traditional stone presses alongside modern equipment. The tours often end with tastings, where you'll discover how to identify quality olive oil by its color, aroma, and taste.

Pairing Olive Oil with Food

Tasting olive oil is much like tasting wine. Start by pouring a small amount into a glass, warming it with your hand, and smelling its aroma. Take a sip, letting the oil coat your palate, and note its flavors—grassy, fruity, or spicy. Pair it with Tuscan bread, and you'll understand why locals treat olive oil as a staple, not just a condiment.

Chianti's olive oil is more than a culinary ingredient; it's a symbol of the region's agricultural heritage. Bringing a bottle home is like capturing a piece of Tuscany's essence.

Picturesque Villages of the Chianti Region

Chianti isn't just about wine and olive oil; it's also home to some of the most charming villages in Tuscany. These hilltop towns and countryside hamlets are rich in history, culture, and scenic beauty, making them perfect for exploration.

1. Greve in Chianti

Often considered the gateway to Chianti, Greve is a lively town with a welcoming atmosphere. Its triangular main square, Piazza Matteotti, is lined with cafes, shops, and wine bars. The Saturday market is a highlight, offering local produce, cheeses, and crafts. Don't miss the Wine Museum (Museo del Vino) for an in-depth look at Chianti's winemaking history.

2. Castellina in Chianti

This medieval town boasts a perfect blend of history and modern charm. Wander through the Via delle Volte, an ancient covered walkway, and enjoy views of the countryside. Castellina is also home to archaeological treasures, including Etruscan tombs that date back thousands of years.

3. Radda in Chianti

Nestled among rolling hills, Radda is a small, picturesque village with narrow streets and stone buildings. Visit the Palazzo del Podestà, a 14th-century town hall adorned with coats of arms. Radda is an excellent base for exploring local vineyards and enjoying quiet moments in nature.

4. Gaiole in Chianti

Known for its proximity to iconic wineries, Gaiole is a haven for wine lovers. The town itself is charming, but its surroundings steal the show. Castles like Castello di Meleto and Castello di Brolio offer history and wine tastings in stunning settings.

5. Panzano in Chianti

Panzano is a food lover's dream, thanks to its world-famous butcher, Dario Cecchini. His lively butcher shop and restaurants serve some of the best meat dishes in Tuscany. Beyond food, Panzano offers breathtaking views and a relaxed atmosphere.

Each village in Chianti has its own personality, but they all share a common thread: a commitment to preserving tradition while welcoming visitors with open arms. Whether you're savoring a glass of wine in a piazza or wandering through cobblestone streets, these villages are where Chianti's soul truly shines.

Chapter 5: Pisa Beyond the Leaning Tower

Piazza dei Miracoli: More Than a Tower

When people think of Pisa, the Leaning Tower inevitably comes to mind. But the Piazza dei Miracoli, or Square of Miracles, is so much more than just its iconic tower. This UNESCO World Heritage Site is a collection of stunning medieval buildings that reflect Pisa's historic prominence as a maritime power and cultural hub.

The Leaning Tower itself, officially the campanile of the Pisa Cathedral, is indeed a marvel. Built in the 12th century, it began to tilt shortly after construction due to unstable ground. Today, thanks to careful engineering efforts, it stands at a stable tilt, drawing millions of visitors eager to climb its 294 steps. However, the square holds even more treasures worth exploring.

The Pisa Cathedral, or Duomo, is the heart of the square. This Romanesque masterpiece, built in the 11th century, is a striking blend of marble, mosaics, and Islamic-inspired arches—a testament to Pisa's rich trade history. Step inside, and you'll find intricate carvings, stunning frescoes, and a pulpit designed by the renowned artist Giovanni Pisano.

Adjacent to the cathedral is the Baptistery of St. John, the largest of its kind in Italy. Its acoustics are legendary; guides often demonstrate its echo by singing a single note that resonates beautifully. The baptistery's elegant design, combining Romanesque and Gothic styles, showcases the artistic evolution of the time.

The Camposanto Monumentale, or Monumental Cemetery, is perhaps the most peaceful corner of the piazza. Legend has it that soil from Golgotha, where Christ was crucified, was brought here, giving the cemetery its sacred atmosphere. Its frescoes, although damaged during World War II, remain hauntingly beautiful, depicting scenes from the Last Judgment and daily medieval life.

Piazza dei Miracoli is a place where history and art come alive. While the tower may steal the spotlight, the other landmarks offer a deeper understanding of Pisa's legacy. Spend a day here, and you'll leave with a newfound appreciation for this city's past.

Walking the Arno Riverbanks

The Arno River is the lifeblood of Pisa, flowing gracefully through the city and offering a serene backdrop for exploration. A walk along its banks is not just a chance to admire picturesque views but also an opportunity to experience Pisa's rich history, vibrant culture, and everyday life.

Start your stroll at Lungarno Mediceo, one of Pisa's most elegant riverfront streets. Lined with grand palaces, such as the Palazzo Medici, this area reflects the city's Renaissance-era wealth and power. Many of these buildings now house museums, universities, or private residences, blending old-world charm with modern-day activity.

As you walk, you'll encounter the Church of Santa Maria della Spina, a tiny Gothic gem perched right on the riverbank. This 13th-century church, once a reliquary for a thorn from Christ's crown, is a marvel of intricate carvings and spires. Its delicate beauty contrasts with the grander structures around it, making it a must-see stop.

Crossing one of Pisa's many bridges, like the Ponte di Mezzo, offers stunning views of the river and the colorful facades of buildings reflecting in the water. If you're visiting in June, don't miss the Luminara di San Ranieri, when thousands of candles illuminate the riverbanks in honor of Pisa's patron saint.

On the southern side of the Arno, explore Lungarno Gambacorti, home to charming cafes and boutiques. This area has a more relaxed vibe, perfect for enjoying a coffee while watching the world go by. Nearby, you'll find the Palazzo Blu, an art and cultural center hosting rotating exhibitions and a permanent collection of works from local artists.

A walk along the Arno isn't complete without venturing into the neighborhoods that line its banks. Each turn reveals something unique, whether it's a hidden courtyard, a lively piazza, or a quiet garden. The river ties these elements together, reminding visitors of Pisa's deep connection to its waterways.

Pisa's Culinary Secrets: Street Food to Fine Dining

Pisa's cuisine is a delightful mix of tradition and creativity, deeply rooted in Tuscany's culinary heritage. While neighboring cities like Florence and Siena often steal the spotlight, Pisa holds its own with a vibrant food scene that ranges from humble street food to sophisticated fine dining.

Street Food Delights

For a quick and authentic taste of Pisa, start with cecina, a savory pancake made from chickpea flour, water, olive oil, and a pinch of salt. It's simple yet satisfying, often served warm and crispy from wood-fired ovens. Try it at local bakeries like Pizzeria Da Nando, where generations of Pisans have enjoyed this classic snack.

Another must-try is panino con porchetta, a sandwich filled with slow-roasted pork seasoned with garlic, rosemary, and fennel. Vendors at street markets or along the Arno often sell this delicacy, and the aroma alone is enough to draw you in.

If you're visiting in autumn, don't miss the seasonal treat of castagnaccio, a chestnut flour cake enriched with raisins, pine nuts, and rosemary. It's a nod to Pisa's rustic culinary traditions and a sweet way to experience the region's flavors.

Traditional Tuscan Fare

Pisa's trattorias and osterias serve up hearty dishes that showcase the region's love for simple, high-quality ingredients. Start with a bowl of zuppa pisana, a vegetable soup thickened with stale bread and drizzled with olive oil. This humble dish is a testament to

Tuscan ingenuity in turning everyday ingredients into something extraordinary.

For seafood lovers, baccalà alla pisana is a must-try. This dish features salted cod cooked in a tomato and garlic sauce, often paired with polenta or crusty bread. It's a reflection of Pisa's maritime roots and the influence of the nearby Tyrrhenian Sea.

Don't leave without trying pappardelle al cinghiale, wide ribbon pasta topped with a rich wild boar ragù. This dish, slow-cooked with red wine and aromatic herbs, is a Tuscan classic that showcases the region's love for game meats.

Fine Dining Experiences

Pisa's fine dining scene combines tradition with innovation, offering unforgettable meals in elegant settings. Ristorante L'Ostellino, located near Piazza dei Cavalieri, is renowned for its creative take on Tuscan cuisine. Their tasting menus feature dishes like saffron risotto with local pecorino cheese or slow-braised beef cheek in Chianti wine.

For a more intimate experience, visit La Buca di San Ranieri, a family-run restaurant that focuses on seasonal ingredients. Their menu changes frequently but often includes specialties like truffle-infused pasta or roasted duck with figs.

Wine lovers will appreciate Pisa's proximity to Chianti and Bolgheri, two of Tuscany's premier wine regions. Many restaurants offer extensive wine lists featuring local reds, whites, and dessert wines like Vin Santo, traditionally served with almond-studded cantucci biscuits.

Farm-to-Table Adventures

For a deeper dive into Pisa's culinary traditions, consider a visit to an agriturismo, or farm stay. These rural retreats offer cooking classes, wine tastings, and meals made with ingredients straight from the fields. Places like Fattoria San Vito provide a glimpse into the region's agricultural heritage while serving up unforgettable meals.

Whether you're nibbling on street food by the Arno, savoring a rustic Tuscan stew, or indulging in a multi-course dinner, Pisa's culinary scene is a journey in itself. It's a chance to taste the city's history, culture, and creativity—all on one plate.

Chapter 6: Lucca – City of 100 Churches

Biking the Renaissance City Walls

Lucca, often referred to as the "City of 100 Churches," is a Tuscan gem that combines rich history with a sense of tranquility. One of the most remarkable ways to explore Lucca is by biking its well-preserved Renaissance city walls. These walls, built in the 16th and 17th centuries, are not just a defensive structure but a living symbol of the city's history, culture, and ingenuity.

The walls encircle the old town, stretching for about 4 kilometers. Unlike many ancient city walls, Lucca's are wide and flat, making them perfect for a leisurely bike ride. They are lined with trees, offering shade during the warmer months, and provide a unique perspective of the city below and the Tuscan countryside beyond.

Starting at Porta San Pietro, one of the gates leading into the historic center, you can rent a bike from one of the many shops nearby. Most rentals are affordable, and the process is straightforward, ensuring even first-time visitors can hop on and start pedaling.

As you cycle, you'll pass through green parklands, ancient bastions, and scenic viewpoints. The walls are divided into sections, each with its own charm. The Bastione San Paolino, for instance, offers stunning views of the nearby mountains, while the Bastione Santa Croce is a peaceful spot often used by locals for picnics and relaxation.

The elevated path gives you a chance to admire Lucca's architectural beauty from above. From this vantage point, the red-tiled rooftops, soaring church towers, and bustling piazzas come into view. Cycling here feels like stepping back in time, with every turn revealing a new slice of history.

For those who prefer a slower pace, there are benches along the way where you can rest and take in the surroundings. If you're visiting in spring, the walls are particularly beautiful, with blossoming trees adding bursts of color to the landscape. Autumn, with its golden hues, offers a different but equally captivating experience.

Biking the city walls is not just a tourist activity; it's a way of life for the people of Lucca.

Families, couples, and friends use this space for exercise, socializing, or simply enjoying the fresh air. Joining them, even for an hour, offers a glimpse into the local way of life.

Churches and Piazzas: A Photographer's Dream

Lucca is often called the "City of 100 Churches," and for good reason. These churches, ranging from grand cathedrals to small chapels, are scattered throughout the city, each with its own story and architectural style. Together, they create a landscape that feels like a living museum, perfect for photography enthusiasts.

One of the most iconic churches is the Lucca Cathedral, or Cattedrale di San Martino. This Romanesque cathedral, with its intricately carved facade and towering campanile, is a masterpiece of medieval architecture. Inside, you'll find treasures like the Volto Santo, a wooden crucifix believed to have been carved by Nicodemus, and the Tomb of Ilaria del Carretto, a stunning marble sculpture by Jacopo della Quercia.

Another must-visit is San Michele in Foro, located in a bustling piazza of the same name. Its ornate facade, adorned with statues of saints and mythical creatures, is a photographer's delight. The church's design, with its mismatched columns and layers of history, provides endless angles for creative shots.

As you wander through the city, you'll come across smaller, less-known churches like San Frediano with its glittering mosaic facade and San Giovanni, which often hosts classical music concerts. These quieter spots offer an intimate look at Lucca's spiritual heritage.

Lucca's piazzas, or squares, are equally captivating. The Piazza dell'Anfiteatro is particularly unique, built on the site of an ancient Roman amphitheater. Its oval shape and colorful facades create a lively yet timeless atmosphere, making it a favorite spot for photos.

Other noteworthy piazzas include Piazza Napoleone, the city's largest square, and Piazza San Michele, where locals gather to sip coffee or chat. Each square has its own character, reflecting Lucca's layered history and vibrant present.

Lucca's Festivals: Music and Medieval Feasts

Lucca's cultural calendar is filled with festivals that bring the city to life, celebrating everything from music to medieval traditions. These events are a testament to the city's love for art, history, and community.

The Lucca Summer Festival is one of the highlights of the year. Held in Piazza Napoleone, this music festival attracts international artists and fans from all over the world. Past performers have included legends like Elton John, Stevie Wonder, and the Rolling Stones. The atmosphere during the festival is electric, with music filling the streets and locals and visitors alike joining in the celebrations.

For classical music lovers, the Lucca Puccini Festival is a must-attend event. Dedicated to the composer Giacomo Puccini, who was born in Lucca, this festival features performances of his operas in stunning venues across the city. Listening to arias from La Bohème or Tosca in the composer's hometown is a truly magical experience.

Lucca's medieval heritage is celebrated during the Luminara di Santa Croce, a religious festival held every September. The event begins with a solemn procession through the city, with participants carrying candles and lanterns. The streets are beautifully illuminated, creating an enchanting atmosphere. The festival concludes with a grand fireworks display over the city walls.

Another medieval-themed event is the Palio di San Paolino, a crossbow competition held in honor of Lucca's patron saint. Participants, dressed in traditional costumes, compete in a historic reenactment that transports spectators back to the city's past.

Food is also at the heart of Lucca's festivals. The Festa di San Zita, held in April, is dedicated to the city's patron saint of flowers. The streets are filled with vibrant floral displays, and local markets offer delicious treats like chestnut flour cakes and fresh pasta.

Whether you're drawn to the music, history, or food, Lucca's festivals provide a wonderful opportunity to experience the city's culture and connect with its people. They are moments of joy and tradition that make this Tuscan city truly unforgettable.

Chapter 7: The Hilltop Charms of San Gimignano

Towers of Time: Medieval Skyline

San Gimignano, known as the "Town of Fine Towers," offers a captivating glimpse into the past. Nestled in the heart of Tuscany, this medieval town is famous for its striking skyline, dominated by towering structures that have stood the test of time. As you wander through its cobbled streets, the sight of these ancient towers, reaching up to the sky, takes you on a journey through centuries of history.

During the 12th and 13th centuries, San Gimignano flourished as an important stop along the Via Francigena, a medieval pilgrimage route that linked France to Rome. Wealthy families in the town built towers to demonstrate their status and power. At one point, there were over 70 towers, creating a formidable skyline visible from miles around. These towers were not just symbols of wealth; they also served as fortifications, protecting the townspeople from invading forces.

Today, only 14 of these towers remain, but they still stand proudly, offering a breathtaking view of the surrounding Tuscan countryside. As you walk through the main streets of San Gimignano, the towers seem to tell their own stories. The tallest of these is the Torre Grossa, which rises to about 54 meters. It's one of the few towers that are open to the public, offering a panoramic view of the town and the rolling hills beyond. Climbing the stairs to the top feels like stepping back in time, and from the top, you can see the vineyards, olive groves, and distant hilltop towns that make this region so quintessentially Tuscan.

The Torre del Diavolo (Tower of the Devil) and the Torre Chigi are among the other notable towers, each with its own story to tell. The town's skyline is still remarkably intact, thanks to strict preservation laws, and walking around San Gimignano feels like walking through a medieval fairytale. The towers, made of stone and brick, are topped with small, pointed roofs, and many still display family crests or symbols that reflect the town's rich history.

While the towers may have served as symbols of wealth and power in the past, they now serve as symbols of endurance and pride. They remind visitors of San Gimignano's history, and climbing them gives you a sense of how life might have been for those who lived in the town centuries ago.

Local Gelato and Artisan Crafts

San Gimignano is famous for many things, but one of its sweetest pleasures is its gelato. The town is home to some of Italy's finest gelaterias, and it has even earned a reputation for having the best gelato in Tuscany. As you explore the winding streets, you'll find a gelato shop around almost every corner, each offering a variety of flavors made with fresh, locally sourced ingredients.

One of the most famous spots is Gelateria Dondoli, which has won numerous awards for its gelato. The gelato here is made with traditional techniques, and the flavors are anything but ordinary. From creamy pistachio to tangy wild berry, every scoop is a refreshing treat. You can also find seasonal flavors like zabaglione, a rich, custard-based gelato made with egg yolks and Marsala wine, or saffron, which adds a uniquely Tuscan twist. The gelato is served in small, hand-crafted cones, which makes the experience feel personal and special.

But gelato is just one of the town's delightful offerings. San Gimignano is also renowned for its artisan crafts. You'll find small shops selling handmade leather goods, pottery, and jewelry, each created with skill passed down through generations. The town has a long tradition of craftsmanship, and many of the artisans still work in small workshops that you can visit.

The Via San Giovanni is one of the best streets to explore if you're looking for artisan goods. Here, you'll find a variety of shops offering everything from intricately designed ceramics to hand-woven textiles. One shop may feature beautifully embroidered linens, while the next might offer colorful pottery with vibrant Tuscan patterns. If you're in the market for leather goods, there are plenty of small boutiques selling handcrafted belts, bags, and wallets.

For a truly unique souvenir, look for local vernaccia wine glassware, which is made using a technique passed down from medieval times. The glass is carefully blown by artisans who have mastered the craft. You'll often find these pieces in the town's most treasured shops, and they make for a wonderful reminder of your visit to this charming hilltop town.

If you're in San Gimignano in the early morning or late afternoon, you may even catch the artisans working. There's something magical about watching a skilled craftsman mold clay into a beautiful bowl or work with leather to create a perfectly finished product. These small, behind-the-scenes moments add depth to your experience of the town, giving you a chance to connect with its creative spirit.

Sunset Strolls Through Vineyards

No visit to San Gimignano would be complete without spending time in the vineyards that surround it. Tuscany's countryside is one of the most beautiful in the world, and the vineyards here produce some of the finest wines in Italy. San Gimignano is particularly famous for its Vernaccia di San Gimignano, a crisp and refreshing white wine that has been produced in the area for centuries.

The best way to experience the vineyards is on foot. Take a leisurely walk through the rolling hills, where the rows of grapevines stretch as far as the eye can see. As you wander, you'll pass stone farmhouses, ancient olive trees, and breathtaking views of the surrounding countryside. The golden light of the late afternoon bathes the vineyards in a warm glow, and the scent of ripening grapes fills the air.

Several local wineries offer tours and tastings, where you can learn about the winemaking process and sample the region's best wines. These tours often include a walk through the vineyards, where you can see the grapes up close and hear about the different grape varieties that grow in the region. Afterward, you can enjoy a tasting of the wines, paired with local cheeses and cured meats. The wines are often served with a view of the vineyards, making the experience even more unforgettable.

One of the most popular walking routes is the Via delle Volte, which leads you through the rolling hills and past several vineyards. This scenic route offers sweeping views of the countryside, and there are plenty of spots to stop and take in the beauty of the landscape. As the sun begins to set, the colors of the landscape shift, and the warm hues of the sunset create a magical atmosphere. The vineyards seem to come alive in the soft, golden light, and the distant sound of birds singing adds to the peaceful serenity of the moment.

As you continue your walk, you'll eventually come to one of the small wineries where you can sample Vernaccia di San Gimignano. This wine has a long history in the region and is known for its crisp, dry flavor with hints of citrus and almond. It pairs beautifully with the local cheeses and charcuterie, making for a delightful end to a perfect day in the Tuscan countryside.

Whether you're a wine connoisseur or just someone who appreciates beautiful landscapes, a sunset stroll through the vineyards of San Gimignano is an experience you'll never forget. The combination of the stunning scenery, the rich history of winemaking, and the peaceful atmosphere of the Tuscan countryside makes it one of the most enchanting parts of the region.

Chapter 8: Val d'Orcia – A Landscape of Poetry

Cypress-Lined Roads and Rolling Hills

Val d'Orcia is an area that seems to be straight out of a dream. Its landscapes have been described in books, poems, and paintings for centuries, and once you see it for yourself, it's easy to understand why. The rolling hills, dotted with quaint farmhouses, vineyards, and olive groves, create a picture-perfect scene that feels timeless.

One of the most iconic features of Val d'Orcia is its cypress-lined roads, which have become symbols of the region. These towering trees, with their slender trunks and dark green leaves, create a striking contrast against the golden hues of the surrounding countryside. The rows of cypress trees stretch endlessly along winding roads, guiding travelers through the hills. Driving or cycling along these roads is one of the most unforgettable experiences in Tuscany. The sight of these trees standing tall against the wide open sky feels like stepping into another world, one that has remained largely unchanged for centuries.

These iconic cypress trees have become synonymous with Tuscany, especially in Val d'Orcia. Many of them were planted in the Renaissance, when the wealthy families of Tuscany wanted to add a touch of grandeur to their estates. Over time, the trees became an integral part of the landscape. Their presence is almost symbolic, as they stand guard over the land, marking the passage of time.

As you journey through the region, the rolling hills unfold in a series of gentle slopes, each offering a new view more breathtaking than the last. The hills are covered in a patchwork of fields—some golden with wheat or sunflowers, others green with vineyards or olive trees. These gentle slopes create a serene and peaceful atmosphere, making it easy to lose yourself in the landscape. Every turn reveals something new, whether it's a distant hilltop town, a picturesque farmstead, or a charming villa hidden amongst the trees.

The light in Val d'Orcia is something special, especially in the early morning or late afternoon. As the sun rises or sets, the landscape takes on a golden glow. The cypress trees, the hills, and the fields all seem to be bathed in this warm, soft light. The landscape changes with the seasons too, with vibrant greens in the spring and summer, rich golds in the fall, and the bare, earthy tones of winter. But no matter the time of year, Val d'Orcia has a beauty that feels eternal.

The quiet beauty of the region makes it easy to imagine that this landscape has inspired countless artists, poets, and filmmakers over the centuries. It's a place that invites reflection and contemplation, and it's no wonder that it's often called a "landscape of poetry." Whether you're simply passing through or spending more time exploring, the roads lined with cypress trees and the rolling hills will leave you with a sense of peace and a deeper connection to the natural world.

Montepulciano and Pienza: Tuscan Gems

Nestled amidst the rolling hills of Val d'Orcia are two of Tuscany's most beloved towns—Montepulciano and Pienza. Both of these towns are full of charm and history, offering a glimpse into the region's rich cultural heritage. While each town has its own unique character, they both capture the essence of Tuscany in their own way.

Montepulciano is perched on a hilltop, offering sweeping views of the surrounding countryside. The town's narrow streets are lined with charming shops, restaurants, and historical buildings, making it a delightful place to explore. The medieval town center is filled with buildings dating back to the Renaissance, giving visitors a sense of walking through history. As you stroll through Montepulciano, you'll come across beautiful squares, impressive palaces, and quaint churches. The Piazza Grande, the town's main square, is a highlight, with its stunning buildings and the imposing Palazzo Comunale.

Montepulciano is also famous for its wine, particularly its Vino Nobile di Montepulciano, which is considered one of Tuscany's finest wines. The vineyards surrounding the town produce grapes that are used to make this exquisite red wine, and many local wineries offer tours and tastings. The wine is rich, full-bodied, and complex, with flavors that reflect the soil and climate of the region. Visiting the wineries is a great way to learn about the winemaking process and sample some of the best wines Tuscany has to offer.

Just a short drive from Montepulciano is Pienza, a town that's known for its Renaissance beauty and its significance in the history of architecture. Pienza is often called the "ideal Renaissance city" because of its careful planning and design. The town was transformed in the 15th century by Pope Pius II, who wanted to create a utopian city that embodied the principles of the Renaissance. The result is a town that feels perfectly balanced, with its central square,

Piazza Pio II, surrounded by elegant buildings and a beautiful cathedral.

One of the main attractions in Pienza is the Duomo, a stunning Renaissance church with a beautiful interior that features works of art by famous Tuscan artists. The town is also known for its local cheese, Pecorino di Pienza, a delicious sheep's milk cheese that's made in the surrounding hills. You can find many small shops selling the cheese, often paired with local wines or honey. Walking through the peaceful streets of Pienza, you'll feel as though you've stepped back in time, surrounded by the beauty and serenity of the Tuscan countryside.

Both Montepulciano and Pienza are examples of the rich cultural heritage of Tuscany. They offer a blend of history, art, and local traditions that make them essential stops for anyone visiting the region. Whether you're admiring the architecture, tasting the wine, or simply enjoying the views, these towns are gems that capture the heart of Tuscany.

Film Locations: Iconic Backdrops of Tuscany

Tuscany has long been a favorite location for filmmakers, and it's easy to see why. The region's stunning landscapes, charming towns, and historic architecture provide the perfect backdrop for a variety of films, from romantic dramas to epic historical sagas. If you've ever seen a film set in Tuscany, you've likely already encountered some of the iconic locations that make the region so special.

One of the most famous films to be shot in Tuscany is "The English Patient" (1996), which was filmed in several locations around the region, including the Abbazia di San Galgano. This ruined abbey, with its dramatic roofless structure and tranquil setting, made for a stunning backdrop in the film. The abbey is located in the Tuscan countryside, surrounded by vineyards and olive groves, and it's a must-visit location for film buffs and history enthusiasts alike.

Another iconic film location is Montepulciano, which served as the backdrop for the vampire saga "Twilight: New Moon" (2009). The town's medieval streets and ancient buildings provided the perfect setting for the fictional town of Volterra, where much of the film takes place. If you visit Montepulciano, you can still see the locations featured in the film, including the Palazzo Comunale and the charming Piazza Grande.

Tuscany has also been featured in several romantic comedies, such as "Under the Tuscan Sun" (2003), which was filmed in various locations around the region, including the Val d'Orcia. The film's portrayal of the breathtaking landscapes, with their cypress-lined roads and rolling hills, captures the essence of Tuscany's beauty. Many scenes were filmed at the charming villa in the film, which has become a popular tourist destination for fans of the movie.

In addition to films, Tuscany has also served as the backdrop for many television shows and documentaries. Its landscapes, rich history, and cultural traditions make it the perfect setting for stories that celebrate the beauty of Italy. The region's timeless appeal continues to attract filmmakers from around the world, and it's no wonder that Tuscany remains one of the most photographed and filmed regions in the world.

Whether you're a film lover or simply someone who appreciates beautiful scenery, visiting these iconic film locations is a great way to connect with the region's cinematic legacy. As you wander through the streets of Montepulciano, visit the Abbey of San Galgano, or take in the views of Val d'Orcia, you'll feel as though you're walking through a movie set, surrounded by the beauty and history that have inspired countless filmmakers.

Chapter 9: The Maremma – Tuscany's Untamed Side

Exploring Nature Reserves and Coastal Trails

The Maremma, located on the southern edge of Tuscany, offers an entirely different side of the region. Known for its untamed landscapes and raw beauty, Maremma is often regarded as one of Tuscany's last frontiers. Here, nature is still very much in control, and the region offers a range of experiences for those who want to explore the great outdoors.

One of the key attractions in the Maremma is its nature reserves. The area is home to several protected zones that showcase its natural beauty, including the Parco Naturale della Maremma, also known as the Uccellina Park. This expansive nature reserve is a paradise for wildlife lovers and hikers. The park covers about 10,000 hectares of land, stretching from the rolling hills to the Mediterranean coastline. It's a place where you can experience Tuscany as it once was—untouched by human hands and brimming with wildlife.

Inside the park, you'll find a mix of habitats, from dense woodlands and wetlands to open plains and dramatic cliffs that drop into the sea. The park is home to a wide variety of animals, including wild boar, deer, and foxes, as well as hundreds of bird species, making it a haven for birdwatchers. The wild horses that roam the park are a truly unique sight. These horses are descendants of ancient breeds, and seeing them gallop freely across the plains is a reminder of the untamed nature of the Maremma.

For those who love hiking or simply want to get lost in nature, the park offers numerous trails that take you deep into the wilderness. There are routes for all levels of hikers, from short walks through the wetlands to longer, more challenging treks through the hills. One of the most beautiful trails leads to Cala di Forno, a secluded beach that is only accessible by foot. The walk to this pristine spot is an unforgettable experience, with views of lush forests and wide-open plains that stretch toward the sparkling Mediterranean Sea.

The coastal trails in the Maremma are another highlight of the region. These paths wind their way along the rugged coastline, offering breathtaking views of the sea and the cliffs below. Along the way, you'll pass through groves of pine trees and scrubland, with occasional glimpses of the pristine beaches that are hidden away from the crowds. Some of the most famous coastal trails include the paths that connect the towns of Talamone and Porto Ercole, which offer panoramic views of the Tyrrhenian Sea.

For those who want to combine hiking with a bit of history, the Parco Archeologico di Baratti e Populonia is a must-visit. This ancient site, located on the coast near Populonia, is home to the ruins of an Etruscan city, and the hiking trails here allow you to explore the remains of ancient tombs, villas, and temples, all while enjoying the spectacular views of the coastline.

What sets the Maremma apart from other parts of Tuscany is its rugged, wild character. The lack of large-scale development means that visitors can experience a Tuscany that feels untouched and pure. The Maremma Regional Park, with its wildlife, trails, and stunning views, is the perfect place to escape into nature, where the beauty of the landscape is matched only by its sense of tranquility and remoteness.

Etruscan Tombs and Medieval Castles

While the Maremma is best known for its natural beauty, the region is also rich in history. One of the most fascinating aspects of Maremma is its connection to the Etruscan civilization. The Etruscans were an ancient people who lived in Tuscany long before the Romans came to power. The area around Maremma was once a thriving part of the Etruscan kingdom, and today, you can visit several ancient tombs and archaeological sites that offer a glimpse into their world.

One of the most significant Etruscan sites in the Maremma is the Necropoli di Sovana, an ancient burial ground that dates back to the 7th century BC. Located in the hills near the town of Sovana, this necropolis is home to a series of tombs carved into the soft tufa rock. These tombs are some of the best-preserved examples of Etruscan burial practices and offer a fascinating insight into the Etruscan belief in the afterlife. Many of the tombs are decorated with intricate carvings, and some even contain remnants of ancient frescoes.

Nearby, you'll find the Etruscan city of Vetulonia, one of the most important centers of Etruscan culture in the Maremma. The town is home to several ancient ruins, including a large Etruscan tomb known as the Tomba della Matuna, which is believed to belong to a powerful Etruscan family. The tombs here are marked by large stone structures, and the remains of ancient homes and temples can also be explored.

In addition to its Etruscan ruins, Maremma is also home to several medieval castles. These castles were built during the Middle Ages, when the region was ruled by various feudal families and noble lords. One of the most famous castles in the area is the Castello di Scarlino, which sits atop a hill overlooking the town of Scarlino and the sea. The castle dates back to the 12th century and offers stunning views of the surrounding countryside and coastline.

Another impressive medieval fortress is the Rocca di Talamone, a fortress located in the coastal town of Talamone. This castle was built in the 16th century to protect the area from pirates and invaders, and it has been beautifully preserved over the years. Visitors can explore the castle's towers and walls, which offer panoramic views of the Maremma coastline.

The presence of these ancient Etruscan tombs and medieval castles gives the Maremma a sense of timelessness. The combination of ancient and medieval history, set against the backdrop of the region's stunning natural beauty, makes this part of Tuscany a fascinating destination for history buffs and curious travelers alike. Whether you're exploring the eerie tombs of the Etruscans or wandering the ramparts of a medieval castle, you'll find yourself immersed in the rich and diverse history of the Maremma.

Wines and Wild Boar: Flavors of Maremma

When it comes to food and drink, the Maremma is a region that surprises and delights. Known for its hearty and rustic cuisine, Maremma offers a unique blend of flavors that are deeply rooted in its history and traditions. One of the defining aspects of Maremma's cuisine is its connection to the land and its wild ingredients.

The region is famous for its wild boar (cinghiale), which is a staple in many Maremma dishes. Wild boar has been hunted in the

Maremma for centuries, and it's often served as the main course in traditional meals. The meat is lean and flavorful, and it's commonly prepared in a variety of ways. One of the most popular dishes is cinghiale in umido, a slow-cooked wild boar stew that's flavored with herbs, garlic, and red wine. The dish is rich and hearty, perfect for the cooler months when the wild boar is in season.

In addition to wild boar, Maremma is also known for its wild mushrooms, which grow in the forests that cover the hills and mountains of the region. These mushrooms are often used to make savory sauces for pasta or to accompany meats like wild boar. The combination of wild boar and mushrooms is a classic pairing in Maremma, and it's a must-try for any food lover visiting the area.

As for drinks, Maremma is home to some of the best wines in Tuscany, with a reputation for producing bold, full-bodied reds. The region is part of the Morellino di Scansano wine-producing area, which is known for its Morellino wine, a Sangiovese-based red that's rich in flavor and aroma. Morellino wines are often paired with the region's hearty dishes, including wild boar, and they complement the flavors of the food perfectly. The vineyards in Maremma benefit from the region's mild climate and fertile soil, producing wines that are smooth, robust, and full of character.

In addition to Morellino, the Maremma is also known for its Vermentino, a white wine that is crisp and refreshing, making it a perfect match for the region's seafood dishes. The coastal areas of Maremma provide fresh fish and seafood that are often served alongside a glass of chilled Vermentino. Many wineries in the region offer tours and tastings, allowing visitors to sample the wines while enjoying the stunning views of the vineyards and the surrounding countryside.

The flavors of Maremma are deeply connected to the land, and the region's food and wine reflect its untamed and wild character. Whether you're enjoying a plate of wild boar stew, sipping on a glass of Morellino wine, or savoring a meal made with fresh mushrooms, the food of Maremma is a true reflection of its heritage and natural beauty. It's a place where the flavors are rich, hearty, and authentic—just like the region itself.

Chapter 10: Elba Island – Napoleon's Tuscan Retreat

Beaches and Crystal Waters

Elba Island, a jewel in the Tuscan Archipelago, is an extraordinary place where nature and history come together. But perhaps the most compelling aspect of Elba is its coastline – a stunning blend of secluded beaches, hidden coves, and crystal-clear waters. For anyone visiting this Mediterranean paradise, the beaches are undoubtedly one of the highlights of the trip.

Unlike some of Tuscany's more crowded coastal spots, Elba's beaches offer visitors an escape into tranquility. The island's coastline stretches for around 147 kilometers, so there's no shortage of places to explore, whether you're looking for a family-friendly beach or a quiet spot to unwind. The waters around Elba are renowned for their clarity and beauty, and it's no surprise that many of the island's beaches have been awarded the prestigious Blue Flag status for their pristine environmental quality.

One of the most famous beaches on Elba is Spiaggia di Sansone, located near the town of

Portoferraio. This beach is often cited as one of the best on the island, thanks to its combination of smooth white pebbles and clear, turquoise waters. The beach is nestled between rugged cliffs, making it a perfect spot for those who want to enjoy both swimming and sunbathing in a peaceful setting. Sansone is also known for its excellent snorkeling opportunities, as the waters here are teeming with marine life. If you're lucky, you might even spot some dolphins or other sea creatures while you take a leisurely swim.

Another beautiful beach to visit is Spiaggia di Cavoli, located on the southern coast of the island. This is one of Elba's most popular beaches, especially in the summer months. With its golden sand and shallow waters, it's an ideal spot for families and swimmers of all ages. The beach is well-equipped with sunbeds, umbrellas, and a few small restaurants, making it an excellent place to spend the day by the sea. While it can get busy during peak season, it's still a charming and welcoming destination for anyone seeking the warmth of the Mediterranean.

For those who prefer a more secluded experience, Spiaggia di Fetovaia is a hidden gem tucked away in a sheltered bay. It's one of the most picturesque beaches on the island, with soft sand and waters that shimmer in shades of blue and green. The surrounding hills provide a stunning backdrop, making this beach perfect for nature lovers. It's a great spot for swimming, relaxing, and even enjoying a picnic away from the crowds. The beach is a bit off the beaten path, so it's best to get there early in the day to secure a good spot.

Elba's waters aren't just about lounging on the beach. The island is an excellent destination for water sports. Whether it's kayaking, windsurfing, or sailing, the clear waters around Elba offer the ideal conditions for these activities. There are many local providers who offer rental equipment and lessons, making it easy for visitors to try their hand at these popular activities. If you're keen on scuba diving, Elba is also known for its impressive dive sites, with numerous underwater caves, wrecks, and rich marine life waiting to be discovered.

Beyond the beaches, Elba's coastline offers plenty of opportunities for hiking, with scenic trails that lead through lush pine forests and along rocky cliffs. These trails offer some of the best views of the island and its crystal-clear waters, making them perfect for nature walks and photography. Many of these coastal routes are relatively easy to navigate, making them suitable for all types of visitors, whether you're an experienced hiker or just looking for a leisurely stroll.

One of the best ways to experience the island's stunning coastline is by boat. Renting a boat or taking a boat tour around Elba allows you to see the island from a different perspective and discover hidden coves and pristine beaches that are only accessible from the sea. There are plenty of options for boat tours, from relaxing day trips to private charters for those who want a more exclusive experience.

With its beautiful beaches, crystal-clear waters, and abundant marine life, Elba Island is a true paradise for beach lovers, water sports enthusiasts, and anyone looking to unwind in a serene coastal setting. Whether you're soaking up the sun on a quiet beach or exploring the island's hidden coves by boat, there's no shortage of ways to enjoy Elba's stunning coastline.

Elba's History: From Napoleon to Today

Elba Island's history is as captivating as its natural beauty, and its most famous chapter involves the exiled French Emperor Napoleon Bonaparte. In 1814, after his first abdication, Napoleon was sent to Elba, where he was granted sovereignty over the island as part of the Treaty of Fontainebleau. Despite his exile, Napoleon didn't spend his time idly; he took immediate steps to improve the island's infrastructure and economy.

Napoleon's presence on Elba was a significant event in the island's history. During his time on the island, he made several changes to Elba's social and political structure. He established a new government and introduced reforms that were aimed at modernizing the island. One of his first tasks was to improve the island's infrastructure. Napoleon ordered the construction of new roads, fortifications, and a more efficient system for managing the island's resources, such as its mining operations. These improvements helped the island thrive during his brief rule.

Napoleon also took an interest in the island's economy, particularly its mining industry. Elba was known for its iron ore deposits, and Napoleon sought to improve the mining techniques used on the island, making it a more profitable industry. He even had plans to expand the ironworks on the island, which later contributed to Elba's reputation as a key supplier of iron in Europe.

Today, you can visit some of the historical sites that are linked to Napoleon's time on Elba. The most famous of these is Napoleon's residence, Villa dei Mulini, located in the town of Portoferraio. This villa served as Napoleon's official residence during his exile, and it's now a museum dedicated to his time on the island. The villa offers a fascinating glimpse into the life of the exiled emperor, showcasing furniture, personal belongings, and artifacts from his stay. Visitors can also explore the gardens surrounding the villa, which offer panoramic views of the island and the sea.

Another significant site linked to Napoleon is the Villa San Martino, which was one of his summer residences. Located just outside Portoferraio, the villa is set in lush gardens and surrounded by scenic landscapes. The villa and its grounds are open to the public and provide a deeper understanding of Napoleon's life on Elba, offering insights into his personal tastes and interests.

After his return to France in 1815, Napoleon's reign on Elba ended abruptly, but his legacy on the island remains to this day. His time on Elba is an integral part of the island's history, and many of the buildings, roads, and fortifications he built can still be seen throughout the island.

While Napoleon's time on Elba was brief, it played a key role in shaping the island's history. Today, Elba is a popular tourist destination, and its historical significance is just one of the many reasons why visitors flock to the island.

Hidden Villages and Coastal Cuisine

One of the most enchanting aspects of Elba Island is its hidden villages. While the island is famous for its beaches and history, it's also home to charming, off-the-beaten-path villages that provide a glimpse into the traditional Tuscan way of life. These villages are often nestled in the hills or perched on the cliffs overlooking the sea, offering stunning views and a quiet escape from the more touristy areas of the island.

One such village is Marciana, a quaint hilltop town that offers a glimpse into Elba's medieval past. Located in the western part of the island, Marciana is known for its narrow cobblestone streets, colorful houses, and peaceful atmosphere. The village is dominated by the fortress of Marciana, which dates back to the

12th century and offers spectacular views of the surrounding countryside. Walking through the village, you'll find charming squares, small cafés, and local shops selling handmade goods, all of which contribute to the town's timeless appeal.

Another hidden gem is Capoliveri, a village located on the southern coast of the island. Capoliveri is famous for its picturesque streets, lined with traditional Tuscan houses and flowers in full bloom. The town is perched on a hill, providing breathtaking views of the coastline and the sea. Capoliveri has a laid-back atmosphere, with quaint trattorias and boutiques where you can enjoy the island's local produce.

Elba's villages are also known for their coastal cuisine, which is deeply rooted in the island's fishing and agricultural traditions. One of the most famous dishes on Elba is cacciucco, a hearty fish stew made with a variety of fresh fish, shellfish, and tomatoes. The dish is flavored with garlic, olive oil, and red wine, and it's typically served with toasted bread. It's a dish that reflects the island's maritime heritage and is a must-try for anyone visiting Elba.

Another local specialty is spaghetti alle vongole, a simple yet delicious dish made with pasta, clams, olive oil, garlic, and fresh herbs. The clams used in this dish are sourced from Elba's clear waters, ensuring that the dish is as fresh as it gets. Elba is also known for its local wines, particularly the Ansonica, a white wine that pairs perfectly with the island's seafood dishes.

For those who want to experience the flavors of Elba in a more authentic setting, the island's family-run trattorias and restaurants offer a chance to sample traditional dishes made with locally sourced ingredients. Many of these eateries are located in the island's hidden villages, providing an intimate dining experience that's hard to find in more touristy areas.

From its hidden villages to its coastal cuisine, Elba Island offers visitors a chance to experience the island's rich traditions and natural beauty. Whether you're exploring the charming streets of Marciana, enjoying a meal in a local trattoria, or simply relaxing by the sea, Elba is a place that captures the heart and soul of Tuscany.

Chapter 11: Arezzo – The Heart of Tuscan Antiquity

Frescoes by Piero della Francesca

Arezzo is a town that holds a unique place in the heart of Tuscany, not only because of its beautiful landscapes and medieval streets but also because of its incredible artistic heritage. Among the jewels of Arezzo's artistic wealth are the frescoes by Piero della Francesca, one of the most influential artists of the Italian Renaissance. These frescoes are not just simple paintings on walls; they are windows into a world of beauty, spirituality, and genius.

Piero della Francesca was a master of perspective, light, and color. His frescoes are iconic not just for their aesthetic brilliance but for how they convey stories with remarkable depth and clarity. If you want to understand the soul of Renaissance art, you must experience the frescoes of Piero, especially the ones housed in Arezzo.

The most famous of these frescoes are located in the Church of San Francesco, particularly in the Legend of the True Cross cycle. This remarkable series of frescoes is considered one of the most important examples of Renaissance frescoes in Italy. It tells the story of the True Cross, the legendary story of how a simple wooden cross became a symbol of Christ's sacrifice.

The frescoes in the Church of San Francesco are remarkable for several reasons. First, there's the sheer scale of the work. The frescoes are large and cover multiple walls, giving viewers a sense of the scope and grandeur of Piero's vision. But what really sets these frescoes apart is the artist's ability to weave together narrative and symbolism. Each scene is filled with rich details, from the intricate costumes of the figures to the expressive faces that show a depth of emotion. Piero della Francesca used light and perspective in a way that was revolutionary for his time. His use of chiaroscuro—the contrast between light and dark—brought a three-dimensional quality to his figures, making them seem as though they could step out of the walls.

The frescoes of the Legend of the True Cross are also notable for their careful use of perspective. Piero was fascinated by the mathematical aspects of art, and he applied his knowledge of geometry to create a sense of depth and space that was ahead of its time. The way the figures in these frescoes seem to interact with their environment, standing or reclining in naturalistic poses, speaks to Piero's mastery of human anatomy and his understanding of how light and shadow shape our perception of the world.

To truly appreciate these frescoes, it's important to spend time looking at the details. The frescoes are rich in symbols, and each element—from the trees in the background to the gestures of the figures—has meaning. The story of the True Cross is not just a biblical narrative; it's a reflection of Christian themes of salvation, suffering, and redemption. And yet, through

Piero's careful attention to the natural world, we see the story told in a way that feels both timeless and deeply rooted in the earthly experience.

In addition to the frescoes in the Church of San Francesco, there are also other works by Piero della Francesca in Arezzo. The Museo di San Salvi, located in the former monastery of the same name, houses several other works by the artist, including altarpieces and smaller paintings. These pieces provide a fuller picture of Piero's development as an artist and his influence on the Renaissance movement.

Piero della Francesca's frescoes in Arezzo are not just for art lovers; they are for anyone who seeks to understand the deep spiritual and intellectual currents that shaped Tuscany during the Renaissance. They are a testament to the power of art to transcend time and connect us with the past. Visiting these frescoes is like stepping into another world—one where beauty, faith, and knowledge come together in a perfect harmony.

Antique Markets and Artisan Treasures

Arezzo is a town with a rich history, and one of the best ways to experience its past is through its antique markets and artisan treasures. Whether you are an avid collector, a history enthusiast, or just someone who appreciates craftsmanship, Arezzo offers a unique opportunity to step back in time and explore its antique shops and markets, where you can find everything from ancient relics to finely crafted modern art.

The most famous of Arezzo's antique events is the Fiera Antiquaria, the town's monthly antique fair. This is one of the largest and most prestigious antique markets in Tuscany, and it has been running for centuries. Held on the first Sunday of every month, the fair draws dealers and collectors from all over Italy and beyond. The Fiera Antiquaria is a labyrinth of stalls, each one filled with treasures from every era of Arezzo's long and storied history.

As you wander through the market, you'll find an incredible variety of antiques on display. There are furniture pieces from the Renaissance, Baroque, and Victorian periods, as well as paintings, sculptures, jewelry, and ceramics. Many of these items come from the local area, offering a rare glimpse into the everyday life of past generations. If you're interested in the Tuscan craftsmanship that shaped the region's identity, this is the place to find original items made by local artisans.

One of the highlights of the Fiera Antiquaria is the jewelry section. Arezzo has been famous for its goldsmithing traditions for centuries, and its artisans continue to produce some of the finest jewelry in Italy. You'll find antique pieces made of gold, silver, and precious stones, as well as modern creations that combine traditional techniques with contemporary designs. Some of the jewelry is so finely crafted that it can be difficult to tell whether it's a vintage piece or a modern reproduction.

In addition to antique markets, Arezzo is also home to a number of artisans who continue to create beautiful handmade goods using traditional methods. These artisans work in a variety of media, including leather, wood, ceramics, and metal. Many of the shops in the town center specialize in high-quality, handmade products, such as leather bags, wallets, and belts, which are made from the finest materials and crafted with great attention to detail.

Arezzo's artisan community is deeply rooted in the region's rich history of craftsmanship. Many of the skills used by today's artisans have been passed down from generation to generation. These craftspeople use time-honored techniques, blending old-world traditions with modern sensibilities to create one-of-a-kind pieces. Whether you're shopping for a unique gift or simply admiring the skill of the craftsmen, Arezzo's artisan shops are an essential part of the town's charm.

Beyond the markets and shops, Arezzo also hosts a number of events and festivals that celebrate the town's craftsmanship and antique traditions. From exhibitions to workshops, visitors can engage with the town's rich artistic heritage and even try their hand at some traditional crafts themselves. For anyone interested in learning more about the local arts and crafts, Arezzo offers an abundance of opportunities to get hands-on with the region's artistic traditions.

Whether you're hunting for a rare antique, exploring the town's artisan workshops, or simply enjoying the lively atmosphere of the antique fair, Arezzo's markets and artisan treasures offer a tangible connection to the past. The history, craftsmanship, and beauty of this wonderful town are on full display in its antique shops and bustling markets, making it a must-visit destination for those seeking a deeper understanding of Tuscany's cultural heritage.

Festivals and Local Traditions

Arezzo, like many towns in Tuscany, is deeply rooted in its traditions, and one of the best ways to experience the local culture is by participating in its festivals. These celebrations, which often date back centuries, provide a fascinating insight into the customs, history, and spirit of Arezzo. Whether they celebrate religious events, historical figures, or local produce, Arezzo's festivals are a vibrant reflection of the town's heritage.

One of the most famous festivals in Arezzo is the Giostra del Saracino, a medieval jousting tournament that takes place twice a year, in June and September. The event dates back to the 16th century and is a thrilling spectacle of knights on horseback, colorful pageantry, and ancient traditions. The Giostra del Saracino takes place in the town's main square, Piazza Grande, where the knights, dressed in medieval armor, ride in a series of jousts against a wooden figure representing the Saracen. This tournament isn't just a display of skill; it's a celebration of Arezzo's medieval past and the town's rich history. The event is also accompanied by music, parades, and festivities, making it a must-see for anyone visiting the town during the summer months.

In addition to the Giostra del Saracino, Arezzo is also known for its religious festivals, which are celebrated with great reverence and joy. The most important of these is the Feast of St. Donatus, the patron saint of Arezzo. This festival takes place on August 7th and is a deeply spiritual event that celebrates the town's connection to its saint. The festival is marked by processions, masses, and special events, all of which honor St. Donatus and his importance to the town.

The town also celebrates several other festivals throughout the year, including the Antique Market, which brings together dealers and collectors from all over Italy to showcase the region's antique treasures, and the Festa della Madonna del Conforto, a celebration of the town's patron saint, which takes place in February and features religious processions, concerts, and special events.

For anyone interested in local traditions, Arezzo's festivals offer a unique way to immerse oneself in the community's culture. These events are not just about entertainment; they are an opportunity to connect with the history and spirit of Arezzo. The town's festivals highlight the important milestones in the town's life, from religious events to historical reenactments, and provide visitors with a chance to participate in the same festivities that have been enjoyed by the locals for centuries.

One particularly charming tradition in Arezzo is the Festa della Bistecca (Steak Festival), which celebrates the region's renowned beef and the culinary traditions surrounding it. Held in the summer, this festival is an invitation to taste some of the finest steaks in Italy, cooked on the grill over an open flame. Visitors can savor the rich flavors of Tuscan meat while enjoying the lively atmosphere of the town's streets, which are filled with food stalls, music, and laughter.

The festival is a great example of how Arezzo's culinary traditions are closely tied to the town's cultural identity.

Arezzo also celebrates Christmas in a way that is uniquely its own. The town is decorated with lights, and special markets spring up in the main squares. The Arezzo Christmas Market is a wonderful place to find local handicrafts, artisanal gifts, and seasonal treats. Visitors can stroll through the charming streets, enjoy a cup of vin brulé (hot spiced wine), and experience the warm, welcoming atmosphere that makes

Arezzo a special place during the holiday season.

In the fall, Arezzo hosts the Corsa della Rocca, a traditional race in which participants compete in a series of challenges that test both strength and agility. This event is a tribute to the town's medieval roots, and it is followed by a grand feast that includes many traditional Tuscan dishes. It's a perfect example of how Arezzo celebrates its medieval heritage while also offering fun and excitement for all ages.

Finally, there is the Arezzo Music Festival, which brings together musicians from around the world to perform in the town's beautiful churches, historic palaces, and open-air venues. This festival showcases Arezzo's vibrant artistic culture and offers a wonderful opportunity to experience live performances in some of the town's most stunning settings. The festival attracts both classical music enthusiasts and those who enjoy more contemporary genres, making it a diverse and inclusive celebration of music in all its forms.

Participating in Arezzo's festivals is an unforgettable experience that gives you a deeper understanding of the town's cultural fabric. Whether you're watching knights joust in the Giostra del Saracino, tasting local steaks at the Festa della Bistecca, or enjoying the religious processions during the Feast of St. Donatus, Arezzo's festivals offer something for everyone. They provide an immersive experience that allows visitors to connect with the town's traditions and its vibrant, living history.

Arezzo is a town where the past and present coexist in perfect harmony. From the remarkable frescoes of Piero della Francesca to the bustling antique markets and the lively festivals that fill the town's calendar, Arezzo offers a window into the heart and soul of Tuscany. It is a town that invites visitors to slow down, take in the beauty, and experience the rich traditions that have shaped this remarkable part of the world for centuries. Whether you are an art lover, a history enthusiast, or someone who simply enjoys the good things in life, Arezzo has something to offer. The town is not just a place to visit; it is a place to feel, to experience, and to remember.

Chapter 12: Livorno – Tuscany's Port City

Seafood and Cacciucco: Livorno's Flavors

Livorno, often overshadowed by its more famous Tuscan neighbors like Florence and Pisa, holds a culinary treasure that is as much a part of its character as the sea itself. This coastal city has a deep connection to its maritime roots, and the food it serves is a direct reflection of this. The most iconic dish of Livorno is Cacciucco, a hearty seafood stew that tells the story of the city's fishing history.

Cacciucco is a dish born out of the hard work of local fishermen, and it has been passed down for generations. It's made with a variety of seafood, including squid, octopus, and different types of fish, all cooked together in a rich, spicy tomato broth. What makes it distinct is the addition of garlic, red wine, and pepperoncino (chili pepper) for heat, creating a deeply flavorful and robust base. Served with toasted bread and drizzled with olive oil, this dish has become synonymous with Livorno itself. When you sit down for a bowl of Cacciucco in one of the city's many seafront restaurants, you're not just tasting a dish; you're experiencing the essence of Livorno's maritime culture.

But Cacciucco is just the beginning. Livorno is also known for a wide array of other seafood dishes that are reflective of the bounty provided by the Ligurian Sea. From grilled fish and fried calamari to seafood pasta and acciughe (anchovies), Livorno's seafood offerings will satisfy any seafood lover's palate. The city's waterfront eateries and markets are filled with the freshest catches, often brought in from the nearby Mediterranean.

Another delicious experience in Livorno is the street food scene, which has become increasingly popular in recent years. Torta di Ceci, a chickpea flour flatbread, is sold in little stalls across the city, usually paired with a glass of local wine. It's a simple yet satisfying snack that captures the simplicity and flavor of Livorno's culinary traditions.

Livorno's food culture is a reflection of its maritime location and its historical role as a port city. The seafood and Cacciucco are not just meals; they are an important part of the city's identity and history. Each dish you try offers a taste of Livorno's past, where the sea and its bounty have shaped the way the people live, eat, and celebrate.

Canals and the Venezia Nuova District

As you stroll through the historic heart of Livorno, you can't help but be struck by the unique atmosphere of the Venezia Nuova district. This charming area of the city is crisscrossed by a network of canals, and walking through it feels like stepping into another world. The canals are the lifeblood of Livorno, providing not only scenic beauty but also a connection to the city's maritime past.

The canals were first built in the 17th century during the reign of the Medici family, and they were meant to help transport goods around the city and into the bustling port. Over time, the canals became a central feature of the city's layout, and today they are one of Livorno's most picturesque spots. The waterway winds its way through the district, flanked by colorful buildings with brightly painted facades and window boxes full of flowers. The canals are dotted with small bridges, and the atmosphere is quiet, peaceful, and full of history.

One of the most striking features of the Venezia Nuova district is the way the canals are integrated into the daily life of Livorno. Locals still use small boats to navigate the waterways, and you'll often see gondolas, or small motorized boats, ferrying people and goods through the canals. This gives the area an undeniable charm, and it's a great place to wander and soak in the sights and sounds of Livorno's past and present.

Walking along the canals, you'll find quaint cafés, art galleries, and boutiques housed in the old buildings. The area is also home to several seafood restaurants, where you can enjoy a meal while watching boats pass by. In the evenings, the district takes on a magical atmosphere, with lights reflecting off the water and locals and tourists alike enjoying a leisurely stroll along the canals.

While the canals themselves are a major attraction, the Venezia Nuova district is also rich in history. The buildings here reflect the city's evolution from its humble beginnings as a fishing village to its rise as an important port and commercial hub. The district's architecture is a mix of medieval, Renaissance, and Baroque styles, creating an eclectic and visually stimulating environment.

A visit to the canals of Livorno is like taking a step back in time while simultaneously being part of the present-day vibrancy of the city. Whether you're admiring the colorful buildings, enjoying a meal at a canal-side restaurant, or simply taking a leisurely walk through the district, the canals are a reflection of the city's identity—a blend of old-world charm and modern liveliness.

Livorno's Role in Tuscany's Maritime Heritage

Livorno's significance in Tuscany's maritime heritage cannot be overstated. The city's position as a key port and its role in both trade and naval history have shaped its character and its influence on the region and beyond. Today, Livorno remains one of Italy's busiest and most important ports, both for trade and tourism, but its history goes much deeper.

Founded in the late 16th century by the Medici family, Livorno was initially conceived as a free port—a place where merchants from all over the world could come and trade freely. This openness to international commerce led to the city becoming a melting pot of cultures and ideas, as merchants from Genoa, Venice, Spain, and even farther-flung places like the Ottoman Empire passed through its docks. The city's role as a port was not just economic; it helped shape the cultural landscape of Tuscany. People from different countries, with different languages, religions, and traditions, settled in Livorno, leaving behind traces of their cultures in the city's architecture, food, and art.

During the 17th and 18th centuries, Livorno's port became the hub of Tuscany's maritime power. The city's strategic location along the Mediterranean made it a vital point for trade and military activity, especially during times of war. The naval fleet of Livorno was a force to be reckoned with, and its shipyards were among the busiest in Italy. The city also played an important role during the Italian Renaissance, with the Medici using the port as a base for expanding their naval reach across the Mediterranean.

Even today, Livorno's port is central to its economy. It serves as a major gateway for goods and travelers, welcoming cruise ships, ferries, and cargo vessels from all over the world. The port continues to serve as a connection between Tuscany and the rest of the world, and it plays a crucial role in maintaining the city's cultural and economic vitality.

One of the most fascinating aspects of Livorno's maritime heritage is its long history of shipbuilding. The Arsenale di Livorno is one of the oldest shipyards in Europe, and it has been the center of the city's naval production for centuries. Today, visitors can explore parts of the shipyard and learn about the importance of shipbuilding to the city's history. The legacy of the shipyard is still visible in the city's naval museums, where you can view models of historic ships and artifacts from Livorno's time as a naval powerhouse.

Livorno's role in Tuscany's maritime heritage goes beyond just trade and military power; it has also been a center for artistic and scientific exchange. In the 17th and 18th centuries, the city attracted some of the best and brightest minds in Europe, who came to Livorno to exchange ideas and conduct research. Livorno's maritime connections allowed it to play a key role in the Renaissance and Enlightenment movements, helping to spread new ideas and technologies across Europe.

In conclusion, Livorno's role in Tuscany's maritime heritage is vast and deeply ingrained in the city's identity. From its origins as a free port to its present-day role as one of Italy's busiest ports, Livorno's maritime legacy continues to shape the city and its people. Whether you're exploring the canals of the Venezia Nuova district, enjoying the fresh seafood that the city is known for, or learning about its history at one of the city's museums, Livorno's maritime past is never far from view. It's a city where the sea has shaped its culture, its economy, and its very soul.

Chapter 13: Tuscan Cuisine and Culinary Experiences

Farm-to-Table Experiences: Agriturismos

Tuscany's deep connection to the land is one of the core aspects of its food culture, and there's no better way to experience this than through Agriturismos—traditional working farms that offer a complete farm-to-table experience. Agriturismos are scattered across the rolling hills of Tuscany, offering visitors the chance to step into the heart of the Tuscan countryside, surrounded by vineyards, olive groves, and fields of wheat, while enjoying authentic, home-cooked meals prepared with ingredients grown on the farm.

The concept of Agriturismos started in the 1980s as a way for farmers to supplement their income by inviting visitors to stay on their properties. Today, these family-run farmhouses offer a wide range of experiences, from cozy bed-and-breakfast stays to full-course meals, often featuring some of the finest produce and meats from the region. It's a true celebration of the local food culture, where every dish is infused with the flavors of the land.

The beauty of Agriturismos is in their simplicity. Guests often sit down for a hearty meal at long wooden tables, surrounded by rustic charm and the peaceful quiet of the Tuscan hills. The menu is seasonal, crafted from what's available on the farm at the time. A typical meal might start with bruschetta made from freshly picked tomatoes and fragrant basil, followed by a rich plate of pasta drizzled with extra virgin olive oil made from the farm's own olives. Main courses often feature roasted meats—perhaps lamb, wild boar, or chicken—that have been raised and prepared with love and care, while desserts like cantuccini and vin santo (a dessert wine) bring the meal to a satisfying conclusion.

The experience at an Agriturismo goes far beyond just eating. Many farms also offer hands-on activities like harvesting grapes, picking olives, or cooking classes where guests can learn the secrets of traditional Tuscan recipes. The opportunity to learn from the people who grow the food you're eating gives you a deeper appreciation of the region's food culture.

Whether you're enjoying a meal in the cozy dining room of an Agriturismo or out on the terrace overlooking the vineyard, the experience is an unforgettable one. You're not just eating; you're connecting with the land, the people, and the time-honored traditions that make Tuscan cuisine so special.

Truffles, Pecorino, and Tuscan Bread

When it comes to Tuscan cuisine, there are a few standout ingredients that truly define the region's culinary identity. Among them, truffles, pecorino cheese, and Tuscan bread hold special significance, and each is worth exploring in depth.

Truffles are one of Tuscany's hidden treasures. These fragrant, earthy fungi grow beneath the soil, often in the roots of oak and hazelnut trees, and are highly prized in Tuscan cooking. While truffle hunting has been practiced in the region for centuries, it's only in recent decades that it's become a major attraction for food lovers and tourists. The tartufo bianco (white truffle) is especially sought after, with its intense, musky aroma that adds depth to a variety of dishes. Whether shaved over a plate of fresh pasta or mixed into a creamy truffle butter, the truffle is a signature ingredient that elevates any meal it touches. In autumn, it's common to see local truffle festivals where visitors can watch expert hunters and their trained dogs track down these elusive treats, while also sampling truffle-infused dishes.

Moving from the forest floor to the dairy farm, Pecorino cheese is another Tuscan culinary gem. Pecorino is a sheep's milk cheese that has been produced in Tuscany for centuries. It comes in a variety of textures, from soft and creamy to firm and aged, each with its own distinct flavor profile. Pecorino Toscano is particularly beloved, known for its smooth texture and slightly nutty flavor. It's commonly used in dishes like pasta alla gricia, a Roman-inspired recipe, and served alongside honey or jam as part of a cheese platter. Pecorino is also fantastic paired with a glass of Chianti, creating a perfect balance between the wine and the cheese's rich, tangy flavor.

Lastly, Tuscan bread is a defining characteristic of the region's cuisine. Unlike many other Italian breads, Tuscan bread is known for being unsalted, which can be surprising to those accustomed to the salted varieties found elsewhere. The absence of salt in the bread was historically a practical choice, as it kept the bread affordable for the common people. The resulting flavor of Tuscan bread is subtly neutral, making it the perfect companion to the robust Tuscan flavors it accompanies. Whether served alongside a hearty soup like ribollita (a vegetable and bean stew) or used to soak up olive oil, Tuscan bread is the unsung hero of many meals.

Together, truffles, Pecorino, and Tuscan bread offer a window into the essence of Tuscan cooking: simple, locally sourced ingredients combined in ways that highlight their natural flavors. These ingredients are not just food;

they're a reflection of the land, the culture, and the centuries of tradition that have shaped Tuscany's culinary landscape.

Cooking Classes: Learn the Tuscan Way

One of the best ways to truly immerse yourself in Tuscan cuisine is by participating in a cooking class. Learning how to prepare traditional Tuscan dishes gives you a hands-on understanding of the region's food culture, and it's an experience that stays with you long after you've left the kitchen.

Cooking classes in Tuscany are offered by a variety of sources, from local chefs to family-run kitchens, and many are held in rustic farmhouses or Agriturismos, where the surroundings themselves add to the experience. A typical cooking class might begin with a visit to a local market or farm, where you'll select fresh, seasonal ingredients for your meal. You'll be guided by a chef, who will introduce you to the key elements of Tuscan cooking, focusing on simple techniques that allow the ingredients to shine.

In a Tuscan cooking class, you might learn to prepare a variety of traditional dishes. The foundation of many Tuscan meals is pasta, and you'll likely get the chance to knead the dough, roll it out, and cut it into traditional shapes like pappardelle or fettuccine. You may even learn to make pasta al cinghiale, a wild boar pasta dish that is a favorite in Tuscany's more rustic areas. Alongside pasta, you'll probably prepare a few side dishes like vegetable soups, grilled vegetables, or a simple Tuscan salad, all highlighting the freshness of local produce.

As you cook, the class will teach you about the importance of quality olive oil, which is a staple in almost every Tuscan dish. Whether you're drizzling it on a salad, using it to sauté vegetables, or soaking it up with a piece of Tuscan bread, you'll discover the rich flavor that good olive oil adds to a meal. The class will also likely touch on how to balance flavors, using herbs like rosemary, sage, and thyme to enhance the dishes you prepare.

Once everything is prepared, the class typically culminates in a shared meal, where everyone sits down to enjoy the fruits of their labor. The joy of cooking and eating together is at the heart of Tuscan culture, and this communal experience will leave you with memories that will last a lifetime. Whether you're learning to make ravioli, wild boar stew, or desserts like cantuccini and vin santo, each class is a journey into the soul of Tuscany.

The beauty of cooking classes in Tuscany is that they offer much more than just recipes; they offer a deeper understanding of the region's culinary philosophy. Tuscany is all about simplicity, seasonality, and tradition, and a cooking class will show you how these principles come together in the kitchen. And, best of all, you'll leave with the skills and knowledge to recreate the flavors of Tuscany in your own home.

Tuscan cuisine is much more than just food; it's a celebration of the land, the seasons, and the people who have cultivated the region for centuries. Whether you're enjoying a farm-to-table meal at an Agriturismo, savoring the truffles, Pecorino, and Tuscan bread that define the region's culinary identity, or immersing yourself in a cooking class, every bite you take is a reflection of the rich history and traditions of Tuscany. The beauty of Tuscan cuisine lies in its simplicity and authenticity, and the experience of enjoying a meal here is an invitation to understand the region in a deeply personal way.

Chapter 14: Festivals and Cultural Celebrations

Tuscan Carnivals and Historical Reenactments

Tuscany is a land that wears its history on its sleeve. This is nowhere more apparent than in its carnivals and historical reenactments, which are as much a celebration of the region's past as they are of its vibrant present. Whether it's the festive parades of colorful costumes or the reenactment of medieval battles, these events give visitors a chance to step back in time and experience Tuscany as it once was.

One of the most famous carnivals in Tuscany takes place in Viareggio, a beautiful coastal town known for its stunning beaches. The Viareggio Carnival, held annually in February or March, is one of the most significant and well-loved events in the region. The streets come alive with enormous, often satirical floats that parade through the town. These floats are known for their intricate designs, often depicting political figures or social issues with a healthy dose of humor. The event draws visitors from across the world, eager to witness the grand processions, music, and dancing that fill the streets.

But while Viareggio's carnival is the most famous, Tuscany is home to many other carnivals that are equally fun and colorful. In Firenze (Florence), you'll find a more traditional carnival, complete with masked balls and lively music. The Mugello region also hosts a smaller, yet equally charming, carnival where locals gather to enjoy food, drink, and dancing.

Alongside the colorful carnivals, Tuscany is also famous for its historical reenactments, which transport you to the medieval and Renaissance periods. One of the most famous historical festivals is The Palio di Siena, a thrilling horse race that takes place in Piazza del Campo, Siena's central square. This race is no ordinary event; it's a centuries-old tradition that pits different neighborhoods, known as contrade, against each other in a fiercely competitive race. The Palio is much more than a horse race—it's a deeply emotional event where the entire city comes together to cheer on their contrade, each with its own unique identity and history.

Another notable historical reenactment is The Calcio Storico in Florence. This centuries-old game, dating back to the Renaissance, is a violent mix of soccer, rugby, and wrestling, played in traditional costumes. It's part of a week-long celebration that culminates in a dramatic match in Piazza Santa Croce, where players represent Florence's historic neighborhoods. Watching these reenactments can feel like stepping into the past, as you witness ancient traditions still alive in the streets of Tuscany.

Whether it's a carnival filled with colorful parades or a medieval battle reenactment, these celebrations are a reminder of Tuscany's rich cultural heritage, and they offer a fun and engaging way for visitors to experience the region's history firsthand.

Wine and Food Festivals Across the Region

Tuscany's wine and food festivals are a feast for the senses, drawing visitors from around the world to sample some of the finest local produce and wines. The region's natural beauty, combined with its incredible culinary traditions, makes it the perfect place to indulge in local delicacies and enjoy a glass of fine Chianti or Brunello di Montalcino. These festivals are a great way to experience the heart and soul of Tuscan culture.

One of the most famous food festivals in Tuscany is the Chianti Classico Wine Festival, held every year in Greve in Chianti. This event is a must for wine lovers. It's an opportunity to taste some of the best Chianti wines directly from the producers themselves. The festival takes place in Greve's charming main square, where dozens of local wineries set up booths to showcase their wines. Visitors can sample a variety of wines, learn about the winemaking process, and purchase bottles to take home. The festival is a celebration not only of the wine but also of the incredible landscapes of the Chianti region, which have been shaped by generations of winemakers.

Another notable wine festival is The Vino Nobile di Montepulciano Wine Festival. Held in the historic town of Montepulciano, this event celebrates the region's famous Vino Nobile wine. The town itself is stunning, perched on a hilltop and offering breathtaking views of the surrounding countryside. During the festival, you can wander through the narrow streets, visit wine cellars, and taste the famous Vino Nobile along with other regional wines. The event is also a great time to enjoy local food, such as pici pasta, wild boar, and other Tuscan specialties.

If you're more inclined toward food than wine, Tuscany has plenty of festivals dedicated to its rich culinary heritage. The Tartufo Bianco Festival in San Miniato, for instance, is a celebration of the region's prized white truffles, which are harvested in the autumn. Truffle lovers can enjoy tasting menus and cooking demonstrations, all centered around this delicious and aromatic ingredient. The festival also offers the chance to buy fresh truffles, truffle-infused oils, and other gourmet products.

In Siena, the Fiera del Cioccolato (Chocolate Fair) celebrates all things sweet. Here, you'll find the best chocolates from across Tuscany and Italy, with vendors offering everything from fine artisanal chocolates to rich truffle-infused treats. For food lovers, there's no better way to indulge in the best of Tuscany's gourmet offerings.

The region also hosts numerous smaller, village-based festivals, often dedicated to specific foods. The Sagra del Cinghiale (Wild Boar Festival) is celebrated in several towns, offering the chance to taste this delicious, hearty meat prepared in a variety of ways, from stews to sausages. Olive oil festivals, such as the one in Cortona, also offer a chance to sample freshly pressed oils, which are a cornerstone of Tuscan cuisine.

These food and wine festivals are much more than just opportunities to eat and drink—they are a way to connect with the region's traditions, its people, and the land. The chance to meet local producers, hear their stories, and learn about their methods adds a personal touch to each festival. Whether you're sipping wine in a historic town square, tasting wild boar in a countryside village, or savoring truffles under the Tuscan sun, you're immersing yourself in the very essence of Tuscany's food culture.

Music Under the Tuscan Sun

Tuscany is not just a place of visual beauty and culinary delights—it's also a place that celebrates music in all its forms. From classical concerts in ancient theaters to jazz festivals set against the backdrop of rolling hills, the region offers a diverse range of musical experiences that attract musicians and audiences from around the world.

One of the most iconic music festivals in Tuscany is the Maggio Musicale Fiorentino in Florence. Founded in 1933, this annual festival is one of the oldest and most prestigious music festivals in Italy. Held during the month of May, it features a wide range of performances, from opera to orchestral concerts and chamber music. Some of the world's top musicians and conductors perform in the magnificent Teatro del Maggio Musicale, as well as in other venues around the city. It's a celebration of classical music in the heart of one of the most culturally rich cities in the world.

For fans of more contemporary music, Tuscany also hosts a range of jazz festivals. One of the most famous is the Lucca Jazz Festival, which attracts jazz lovers from all over the world. The festival features performances by both established and up-and-coming jazz artists, and it takes place in the beautiful, historic town of Lucca. The festival is a wonderful blend of music and the Tuscan landscape, as many concerts are held in outdoor venues, such as piazzas and gardens, creating a magical atmosphere under the stars.

Tuscany's rich musical traditions aren't just limited to large festivals; there are also smaller, local performances that are equally charming. In Siena, for example, you can enjoy medieval music played on period instruments, which provides a glimpse into the sounds of the past. Similarly, in the hill towns of Tuscany, you might come across small ensembles performing in intimate settings, such as village squares or vineyard terraces. These performances capture the essence of Tuscany's cultural landscape, blending music with the beauty of the natural surroundings.

Tuscany is also known for its beautiful music venues, including the Teatro del Opera in Florence, the Teatro di San Carlo in Naples, and Teatro Comunale in Bologna, all of which host world-class performances.

Tuscany's festivals and cultural celebrations are a reflection of the region's rich history, vibrant culture, and deep connection to the land. From lively carnivals and historical reenactments to food and wine festivals and music under the stars, these events offer a unique opportunity to immerse yourself in Tuscany's spirit. Whether you're a lover of food, wine, history, or music, there's something for everyone in Tuscany's bustling festival calendar. By participating in these celebrations, you not only get to experience the best of Tuscan culture but also become part of its living, breathing tradition.

Chapter 15: A Guide to Tuscan Itineraries

One Week in Tuscany: The Essentials

Tuscany is a region rich in history, art, food, and breathtaking landscapes. While one could spend months exploring all it has to offer, a week in Tuscany can still provide a fulfilling experience, combining the essential highlights with a few less-known gems. Here's how you can make the most of seven days in this enchanting region.

Day 1: Florence – The Heart of Tuscany

Begin your Tuscan adventure in Florence, the region's capital and a city synonymous with the Renaissance. Spend your first day wandering through the historic center, taking in the awe-inspiring architecture. Visit the Duomo, the Uffizi Gallery, and the Accademia, where Michelangelo's David awaits. Stroll along the Arno River, cross the famous Ponte Vecchio, and relax in the Piazza della Signoria. In the evening, enjoy a leisurely dinner in one of the city's excellent Trattorias, sampling classic Tuscan dishes like Bistecca alla Fiorentina (Florentine steak) and Ribollita (a hearty vegetable soup).

Day 2: The Tuscan Countryside – Chianti Region

On your second day, leave Florence behind and head towards the rolling hills of the Chianti region. Known for its scenic vineyards and charming villages, this area is the perfect spot to enjoy a wine-tasting tour. Stop by a few local wineries, learn about the famous Chianti Classico wine, and enjoy tastings accompanied by local cheeses and olive oils. Afterward, explore the medieval town of Greve in Chianti and take a walk through the vineyards, perhaps even enjoying a picnic amidst the hills. Finish the day with a visit to Castellina in Chianti, where you can wander through quaint streets and experience the essence of rural Tuscany.

Day 3: San Gimignano and Volterra – Timeless Hilltop Towns

The third day of your journey will bring you to two of Tuscany's most captivating medieval towns: San Gimignano and Volterra. San Gimignano, known for its tower-filled skyline, is often referred to as the "Medieval Manhattan." Walk through its narrow streets, explore its historical buildings, and sample the renowned vernaccia wine. After lunch, head to Volterra, a stunning hilltop town that feels like it's frozen in time. Visit the Etruscan Museum, the Roman Theater, and the Palazzo dei Priori. The charm of Volterra is in its quiet streets and the spectacular views of the surrounding countryside.

Day 4: Siena – The Heart of Medieval Tuscany

No trip to Tuscany is complete without a visit to Siena, a medieval gem that still retains much of its old-world charm. Start your day in Piazza del Campo, the main square, and don't miss the Duomo di Siena, a magnificent cathedral known for its marble facade and intricate interiors. Walk through the narrow streets, stopping to admire the Gothic architecture and visiting local shops for handmade crafts. If your visit falls in the summer, the Palio di Siena, a thrilling horse race held twice a year, is an experience not to be missed. In the evening, enjoy a hearty meal at a local osteria, savoring dishes like pici pasta or wild boar stew.

Day 5: Val d'Orcia – Tuscany's Iconic Landscape

Day five takes you to the stunning Val d'Orcia, a region that captures the quintessential image of Tuscany with its cypress-lined roads and rolling hills. Drive through Pienza, a town famous for its Pecorino cheese, and enjoy the views from

Monticchiello and Bagno Vignoni, a village famous for its ancient thermal baths. Stop by Montepulciano for a wine-tasting session and stroll through its beautiful medieval streets. The Val d'Orcia is also a UNESCO World Heritage Site, and its landscapes have served as the backdrop for countless films, making it one of the most photographed areas in Tuscany.

Day 6: Pisa and Lucca – Iconic Landmarks and Hidden Charms

On your sixth day, head to the western part of Tuscany to explore Pisa and Lucca. Start with a visit to the famous Piazza dei Miracoli in Pisa, home to the iconic Leaning Tower of Pisa. But beyond the tower, there's much more to see, including the Duomo di Pisa and the Campo Santo. Afterward, take a short drive to Lucca, a charming walled city filled with Romanesque churches and historic squares. Rent a bike and ride around the city's Renaissance-era walls, or simply wander the picturesque streets and enjoy the relaxed atmosphere. Lucca is also known for its delicious pastries, so be sure to stop for a treat before heading back.

Day 7: The Maremma – Tuscany's Coastal Beauty

End your week in Tuscany with a visit to the Maremma region, a coastal area known for its rugged landscapes, wild nature reserves, and charming towns. Take a walk through Parco della Maremma, a nature reserve that offers pristine beaches, wildlife, and the chance to see the Maremma horses. Visit Pitigliano, an ancient town built into the rock, and Saturnia, famous for its natural hot springs. If you're looking for a relaxing end to your trip, consider a visit to one of the region's beautiful beaches, such as Cala Violina or Castiglione della Pescaia, before enjoying a seafood dinner by the sea.

Off the Beaten Path: Hidden Treasures

While Tuscany's major cities and attractions are certainly worth visiting, the region is full of hidden treasures that are often overlooked by tourists. These lesser-known spots provide a more authentic and peaceful experience of Tuscany.

Start your off-the-beaten-path adventure in the Casentino Valley, a lush area in the Arezzo province. This picturesque valley is home to forests, ancient castles, and small villages that are perfect for hiking and exploring. A visit to the Eremo di Camaldoli, a peaceful monastery tucked away in the forest, is a highlight for anyone looking to experience the spiritual side of Tuscany.

For art lovers, the Val di Chiana region, especially the town of Cortona, offers a quieter alternative to Florence. This ancient town boasts stunning views and a rich history, with art galleries and museums that house works by famous artists like Fra Angelico. The nearby Lake Trasimeno provides a beautiful setting for a peaceful afternoon.

The Garfagnana region, located in the Apennine Mountains, offers hiking trails and picturesque villages like Barga and Castelnuovo di Garfagnana. These lesser-visited towns allow you to experience the unspoiled beauty of the Tuscan countryside, far from the crowds of major tourist destinations.

Finally, head to Monte Amiata, a dormant volcano surrounded by forests and charming medieval villages. This region offers spectacular views, beautiful hikes, and the opportunity to visit ancient towns like Abbadia San Salvatore and Arcidosso.

Luxury Tuscany: Exclusive Stays and Experiences

Tuscany is synonymous with luxury, and for those seeking an indulgent experience, the region has plenty to offer. Start by staying in a luxury villa or historic castle. Many of Tuscany's old estates have been transformed into exclusive boutique hotels or agriturismos, offering world-class amenities, private pools, and exquisite views of the countryside.

For an unforgettable experience, consider spending a night in Castello di Velona, a 5-star luxury resort set within a medieval castle overlooking the Val d'Orcia. The castle's spa, wine cellar, and beautiful views make it a dream destination for anyone seeking both relaxation and indulgence.

Tuscany is also home to several luxury wineries, where you can book exclusive tours, enjoy private wine tastings, and even learn how to pair wines with gourmet meals. The Antinori Winery near Florence is one of the most renowned, offering private tastings and tours of its state-of-the-art facilities. In the Chianti region, many wineries offer bespoke experiences, including truffle hunting, cooking classes, and even private dinners in centuries-old cellars.

For those looking to experience a unique adventure, Tuscany's hot air balloon rides offer a thrilling way to see the region's iconic landscape from above. Float over the rolling hills, vineyards, and medieval towns, and enjoy the peaceful serenity of the Tuscan countryside.

Whether you're spending a week in Tuscany or just a few days, the region offers an abundance of experiences that cater to all interests. From the essential must-see cities to hidden gems and luxury experiences, Tuscany is a place where time slows down, and every corner holds something beautiful. Whether you're visiting for the first time or returning to explore more, these itineraries will help you make the most of your time in one of the world's most enchanting regions.

Chapter 16: Farewell Tuscany

Reflections on the Tuscan Spirit

Tuscany is a place that leaves an indelible mark on your heart. Whether it's your first time or your fifth, there's something timeless about this region that makes you feel as though you've discovered a home away from home. As you wander through the vineyards, meander through medieval villages, or relax in a sun-drenched café, Tuscany doesn't just welcome you — it captures you.

The Tuscan spirit is one of simplicity and warmth, woven through every aspect of daily life. It's in the slow rhythms of a rural countryside, where time seems to stretch out as you walk past cypress-lined roads, the sound of church bells ringing in the distance. It's in the way the locals greet you with a smile, eager to share their food, culture, and stories. It's in the hills that stretch endlessly under an expansive sky, creating an overwhelming sense of peace and belonging.

Tuscany has a way of connecting you to the past and the present simultaneously. It's impossible not to feel the weight of centuries of history as you walk through Florence, or the sense of being part of something eternal as you stand at the Piazza del Campo in Siena. But it's also in the daily moments — the enjoyment of a glass of Chianti, the taste of fresh pecorino cheese, and the relaxed pleasure of enjoying the Tuscany sunset over rolling hills. There's a timelessness here, as if the land itself breathes the essence of the region's spirit.

One of the most striking aspects of Tuscany is its celebration of life. It's not about rushing or hurrying; it's about savoring each moment, whether that's through the slow enjoyment of a delicious meal or a leisurely afternoon spent in the countryside. The culture here encourages you to pause, appreciate the beauty that surrounds you, and be fully present in the now.

In a way, Tuscany doesn't just offer scenic beauty and rich culture — it offers a way of living. It's about appreciating the simple pleasures, being connected to the land, and forging relationships with people and places that feel like they've been with you forever. As I reflect on my time in Tuscany, I realize that the Tuscan spirit isn't just something you experience; it's something you carry with you long after you leave.

Must-Know Tips for Future Travelers

As you begin to plan your own Tuscan journey, here are a few essential tips to help you make the most of your time in this enchanting region.

1. Take Your Time: Tuscany isn't a place to rush through. The beauty of the region lies in the

slow pace of life. Don't feel the need to tick off every sight in a day. Spend time in small villages, wander through quiet streets, and enjoy the serenity that makes Tuscany unique.

2. Stay Off the Beaten Path: While cities like Florence and Pisa are certainly worth visiting, Tuscany is filled with hidden gems that most tourists overlook. Venture into the Tuscan hills, visit towns like Cortona or Pitigliano, and explore quieter corners of the region. You'll be rewarded with fewer crowds and a more authentic experience.

3. Don't Skip the Food: The cuisine is one of Tuscany's most defining characteristics. From hearty soups like ribollita to wild boar stew, the food here is rich in flavor and tradition. Be sure to try local specialties and visit agriturismos (working farms) where you can enjoy freshly prepared meals made with local ingredients.

4. Plan for the Seasons: Tuscany's climate can vary dramatically from season to season. Summers can be hot, especially in inland areas, while winters can be chilly, especially in the hills. The spring and fall are ideal times to visit — the weather is comfortable, and the

landscapes are at their most vibrant. If you visit during the harvest season in late summer or early fall, you'll also be treated to grape harvests and olive oil tastings.

5. Learn the Local Etiquette: The Tuscan people are known for their warmth and hospitality, but it's important to remember a few cultural norms. For example, in many small towns, shops may close for a few hours during lunch, so plan accordingly. Also, when dining, it's common to eat in courses, so don't rush through your meal — savor every bite.

6. Rent a Car (But Know When to Park): Tuscany is best explored by car, especially if you want to visit remote villages or travel through the countryside. However, many small towns have narrow streets and limited parking, so be mindful of where you park, and always be patient when driving through winding roads.

7. Respect the Land: Tuscany's natural beauty is one of its greatest treasures, so make sure to respect the environment. Stick to marked trails when hiking, be mindful of your litter, and always seek to leave the landscape as pristine as you found it.

8. Don't Forget the Wine: Tuscany is one of the world's most famous wine regions, so make sure to sample the local wines. Be sure to try Chianti, Brunello di Montalcino, and Vino Nobile di Montepulciano — and if possible, visit a local winery to learn about the wine-making process.

My Final Thoughts: Why Tuscany Will Always Call Me Back

As my journey through Tuscany comes to a close, I find myself overwhelmed with gratitude. There's something about this place that stays with you, something that lingers long after the last glass of wine is finished and the final sunset has faded. Tuscany has a way of weaving itself into your soul, creating a longing for its rolling hills, its ancient villages, its flavors, and its people.

What is it about Tuscany that draws you back, again and again? It's hard to pinpoint exactly, but I think it has to do with the simple way of life, the slower rhythm of time that allows you to truly experience everything the region offers. It's the feeling of being grounded in the present while also feeling connected to centuries of history and culture. Tuscany is not just a place you visit; it's a place that becomes part of who you are.

There's a certain magic in the air here, something that calls you to return, to explore deeper, to experience more. Maybe it's the charm of the small towns that feel like they've been frozen in time. Maybe it's the warmth of the people, always ready to share their love for their land. Or maybe it's the intoxicating beauty of the landscapes, where every turn offers a new view that takes your breath away.

For me, Tuscany will always be a place I return to, whether physically or in spirit. The memories of the long walks through vineyards, the quiet moments in cafés, and the lively conversations with locals will stay with me forever. Tuscany isn't just a destination; it's a part of my journey that I will carry with me, always.

No matter how many places I visit, Tuscany will always hold a special place in my heart, and I know I will be back. For now, though, I say arrivederci — but not goodbye. Tuscany, you will always call me back.

Maps & Travel Routes

Florence

Arno

Chianti Colli Fiorentini

A1 Autostrada

San Casciano Val di Pesa

Montespertoli

Greve in
Chianti

Panzano

Chianti
Classico

Chianti
Colli
Aretini

SR222

The Chiantigiana

Castellini
in Chianti

MAP
OF
CHIANTI

Gaiole in Chianti

Chianti
Colli
Senesi

MAP © 2023, JAMES MARTIN

Siena

Rail Map of Tuscany

Massa

Prato

Pistoia

Lucca

Pisa

Florence

Livorno

Arezzo

Siena

Grosseto

Tuscany
Provinces

Explore Places to Go and Things to See in

Tuscany

Scan the QR code above

Recommended Resources & Acknowledgments

Recommended Resources

As you prepare to embark on your own Tuscan adventure, there are a few resources that can enhance your experience and provide deeper insights into this beautiful region. Here are some of the best ways to further immerse yourself in the wonders of Tuscany:

1. Guidebooks and Travel Guides:

Rick Steves' Italy: Rick Steves offers a great introduction to Italy, with a focus on Tuscany. His guidebook provides tips on how to travel with ease, find the best spots, and discover hidden gems.

Lonely Planet Tuscany: This guidebook is perfect for those looking for comprehensive information on attractions, accommodations, and local advice. Lonely Planet's Tuscany guide is known for its accuracy and practical travel tips.

The Rough Guide to Italy: With in-depth information on Italy's regions, including

Tuscany, this guide is perfect for travelers looking for a deeper dive into the culture, history, and geography of the area.

2. Websites and Online Resources:

Visit Tuscany (visittuscany.com): The official website of Tuscany's tourism board, it offers an abundance of information about attractions, itineraries, and events happening throughout the region.

Walks of Italy (walksofitaly.com): This website offers walking tours throughout Tuscany, providing the chance to explore Florence, Siena, Pisa, and other towns in a more intimate and knowledgeable way.

Tuscan Wine Tours (tuscanwinetours.com): For wine enthusiasts, this site offers a selection of tours and experiences at the best wineries in Tuscany, including Chianti, Montalcino, and Montepulciano.

3. Local Tuscan Cookbooks:

"The Silver Spoon": Considered the bible of authentic Italian cooking, this cookbook offers a wealth of traditional Tuscan recipes to bring the flavors of Tuscany into your kitchen.

"Tuscany: The Beautiful Cookbook" by Lorenza de' Medici: Filled with recipes and photographs, this book will give you a glimpse into the Tuscan way of eating, from hearty stews to delicate pastries.

4. Documentaries and Films:

"Under the Tuscan Sun": While fictional, this film beautifully showcases the Tuscan landscapes, making it a great starting point for anyone curious about the region's charm.

"The Italian Job": Although not primarily focused on Tuscany, this film offers glimpses of Italy's breathtaking countryside.

"Tuscany: The Heart of Italy" (PBS Documentary): For those who want to explore the history, culture, and natural beauty of Tuscany, this documentary is a fantastic resource.

5. Podcasts and Audio Resources:

The Tuscan Traveler Podcast: A fantastic resource for anyone planning a trip to Tuscany, offering insights on local history, wine, food, and travel tips.

Untold Italy Podcast: This podcast features various Italian regions, with a focus on Tuscan culture, food, and places to visit.

Acknowledgments

Creating this guide to Tuscany has been a journey of its own, and I am deeply grateful to all those who contributed to making it a reality. A special thank you goes to:

The Tuscan Locals: Over the years, I have had the privilege of meeting and getting to know the people of Tuscany. From the passionate chefs and vineyard owners to the artisans and tour guides, your warmth and generosity have shaped my understanding of this remarkable region. You've made Tuscany feel like home.

The Historians and Experts: Thanks to the historians, archaeologists, and guides who have shared their vast knowledge of Tuscany's rich past. You've brought the Etruscans, Romans, and Renaissance masters to life in ways that continue to inspire me.

Tuscany's Vineyards and Agriturismos: To the hardworking men and women behind the region's wineries and rural farms, your commitment to tradition and quality has always been an inspiration. Thank you for your hospitality and the opportunity to enjoy the fruits of your labor.

Travel Bloggers and Writers: To the many writers who have documented their own journeys through Tuscany, your blogs and articles provided the inspiration to start this guide and continue to explore the region with fresh eyes.

My Family and Friends: Thank you for your patience, support, and encouragement throughout this process. You've helped me stay grounded and reminded me why I began this journey in the first place.

About the Author

Andra Miles is a seasoned traveler and writer with a deep affection for Italy, particularly its heart and soul — Tuscany. With decades of experience exploring the region, Andra has become a trusted guide to those seeking an authentic Tuscan experience. Her love for Tuscany started many years ago and has grown into an enduring passion, one that she now shares with others through her books, travel guides, and articles.

Andra's writing is a reflection of her own journey — one rooted in curiosity, exploration, and appreciation. Whether strolling the streets of Florence, sipping wine in Chianti, or discovering hidden gems in small Tuscan towns, she has made it her mission to uncover the beauty and charm of the region. Her goal is to help readers experience Tuscany not just as tourists, but as travelers who are deeply connected to the land, the people, and the culture.

In addition to Tuscany, Andra is the author of numerous other travel guides, each written with the same passion for discovery and a desire to bring readers closer to the places that have touched her heart. When not writing, she can often be found in a cozy café, notebook in hand, planning her next adventure.

Notes

Made in United States
Orlando, FL
30 March 2025

59979161R10157